# the Voyage of the Sierra Sagrada:
# Across the Atlantic in a Canoe

# the Voyage of the Sierra Sagrada: Across the Atlantic in a Canoe

Francis Brenton

HENRY REGNERY COMPANY · CHICAGO

# CONTENTS

# the Voyage of the Sierra Sagrada:
# Across the Atlantic in a Canoe

# Chapter I

THE IDEA of crossing the Caribbean in a canoe came to me on the spur of the moment. I suppose most good ideas are like that. They are probably there—in the back of our minds—all the time, and all it takes is a catalyst to allow them to swing into action. A small red-hued fishing canoe, nestling in the yellow coral sand on one of Santa Marta's lazy beaches. Such was the catalyst that started me on the *Sierra Sagrada* journey.

This particular canoe stood out from the others. When I came close to it, I could see it was new. The top rims of fishing canoes always become splintered, for this is where most of the pressures and injuries are taken as nets and spears are dragged over the side. This canoe *was* new, yet it was so full of sand that I was not sure whether or not it had a fault in it. All I could do was furtively inspect the vulnerable places, at the bow and stern, where the center of the tree trunk is liable to have *borrach*—the fatal dry rot that affects so many dugout canoes.

"Who does it belong to?" I asked a promenading beach-comber.

1

I was directed to Anibel Yanes's house—an easy place to find, for it was the only substantial hut on a promontory overlooking the horseshoe-shaped bay.

"*Gracias, señor,*" I thanked my informer, as I was introduced to Anibel Yanes himself.

"There is not much of a life for a fisherman in these parts," Yanes told me, when I inquired if the canoe was for sale.

"I want it for a museum in Chicago," I told him. "And I hope to sail it over there myself."

Anibel showed a great deal of interest at this. "I hate the sea. I get seasick all the time," he told me. "But I would like to come along with you, and then it would be much safer."

I had heard this story before, and I am the first to admit that it is tempting to accept the offer of company. But practice has made me wary.

"I prefer to sail alone," I reluctantly told him. And then I went on to the reason for my visit. "The only thing I insist upon is that the craft be strong, and your canoe looks very strong to me."

"It is indeed," Yanes elaborated. "It is made from the caracoli tree—a tree of great height and strength, and one that will not rot and weaken in salt water."

I knew the caracoli. A tree of the cashew family, it grew in primordial jungles to a height of 150 feet. The unbuttressed trunk often reaches fully 50 feet bare of weakening limbs or branches, and it as likely would have a steady diameter of five to six feet, above the basal swelling. The thick trunk diameter and the long smooth grain made the caracoli perfect for carving and canoe-building.

"How old is it?" I asked Anibel.

"Less than six months old," he assured me, telling me

that it had been built for the nearby Cienega swamplands
less than a year before.

"Did you build it yourself?" I wanted to know.

He laughed shortly. "These are built by generations
of canoe-carvers," he told me. And I took it for granted that
the local craftsmen had a good reputation in the area.

We followed a short path down to the beach, and Anibel
made no excuses about wanting to sell the craft. "I have
not used it for at least a month," he said.

"But surely you can't get seasick on these calm waters?"
I asked, for the sea was presently as smooth as glass, and
even shrimp could be seen quite clearly as they threaded
their way past the few small, round stones that glinted
half a fathom under the tepid surface.

"No," he said, "I don't get seasick when the weather is
like this, but I don't care to work under the hot sun all day
when the jungle's shade is so close."

Anibel was a farmer at heart. I noticed he did not have
the usual callused hands of the fisherman—a characteristic easy to recognize when one had traveled the river
systems and waterways of South America for the previous
two years, as I had done in my usual occupations as photog-
rapher, collector and trader. Anibel's splayed black feet
were of the land and jungle.

But if I could get Anibel's canoe, my plans were only
just beginning to be fulfilled, because my intention was to
buy *two* dugout canoes. Then, when I had formed them
into a rough catamaran, small sails would take me the
1,300 miles to Louisiana from Colombia. And from New
Orleans I would make my way up the Mississippi, to
Chicago. I envisioned a long and easy sail, for in four days it
would officially be spring, and I could hope for good
weather all the way.

I had no more than 600 dollars in my pocket as I talked with Anibel. But I was sure this was more than sufficient to build my own boat and buy adequate stores and equipment.

"How much money do you want for the canoe?" I asked Anibel.

"Two thousand pesos," Anibel said without reservation.

Two thousand pesos was not a great deal of money—only $97 at the present rate of exchange—and I could certainly afford it.

Anibel saw me hesitate and drew the wrong conclusion. "It was a very good tree," he explained. "And 2,000 pesos is exactly the price I paid for it six months ago."

I had no doubt he was telling the truth. My hesitation stemmed from the fact that the canoe was worth much more. Relief at the thought that my tight budget was still being met had temporarily made me speechless.

"It's a deal," I said, and we walked along the simmering beach into Santa Marta city to call on the municipal clerk and make the deal legal.

I had been lucky to have found such a seaworthy craft so fast, for I had had doubts and reservations about the feasibility of taking a dugout canoe into open waters. In the back of my mind I could recall a suchlike craft I had once been riding on a rocky tributary of the Rio Guapore, in Brazil. Two of us had been guiding our way downstream, fending-off rocks in a turbulent mountain current, which was still freshly swollen from a sudden, heavy cloudburst.

"We'll make it easily," my Indian friend had said, as he sat, paddle in hand, in the bow, while I helped steer from the stern.

Then, without warning, there had been a dip in the

water, and we had nose-dived directly into a mid-current boulder. Nine times out of ten one just makes a glancing pass when these things happen. But this time we struck dead center, and even as I was being thrown forward, I saw the canoe split wide open from bow to near amidships, as neat and clean as though we had been sliced by an ax.

Having canoes split in two is an occupational hazard, I later learned, though it seldom happens when the craft is in the water and wet. Still, as I talked with Anibel, I did have some subconscious trepidation as we made our way into the center of Santa Marta. I just hoped it would not happen to Anibel's canoe.

Santa Marta is one of Colombia's more conservative cities. But I was not here to sight-see, and we went straight to the municipal building where miscellaneous public transactions are officiated. Half a dozen stairs up to the office, varnished hardwood swing doors, scratched fogged-glass panels, a heavy paper-stacked desk, three wooden chairs—I think all South American government offices are built on identical lines. To complete the picture, a harassed official, dressed in office suit, white shirt and tie, sat behind his desk, his elbow on a blotter pad, busily scribbling out notes and talking into a bulky black phone.

We did not have long to wait. The idea that a stranger would want to buy a canoe aroused the curiosity of the clerk, and he terminated his phone call in somewhat less time than the regulation three minutes.

Maybe some of his family were in the fishing business. "When you catch a lot of fish, the prices fall," he warned me. "When the prices are high, it is because there are no fish."

"No problem," I assured him. "I did not buy it to go fishing."

It surprised me how often I had to say this. It seems as though a lot of people were anxious that I did not join an already competitive market.

On official stamped paper the receipt was made out:

> I, Anibel Yanes, cedula number 1/681/107 [identity number 1681107], of Santa Marta, sell to Francisco Brenton, holder of British passport C.335532, one rowing canoe with a length of eleven varas by one-meter beam [26 feet long, 40 inches beam]. It is my property, in good shape and condition, and the price for the sale is two thousand pesos.
>
> I hereby declare I have received the money, and am satisfied with the transaction.
>
> Signed, March 17, 1966
>
> El Vendador      El Comprador
>
> Anibel Yanes A    Francisco Brenton

With this solemn ceremony, I became a duly recorded official canoe-owner. The clerk was as starchy as his collar, and he refused to unbend. Politely, he now called me "Captain." In deference, I called him "Your Honor." In actual practice I was still only a canoe-owner, and he was only a clerk. With propriety we bowed to each other, and he offered me an ink-stained hand to shake.

Anibel was already making plans to buy a piece of land as a *finca*, with visions of a small farm, a pleasant river running alongside, a dog or two to go hunting, a small hut, his family—a jungle life free of town-bound chores. He had already worked everything out in detail. His eagerness to go with me to Louisiana evaporated.

"I almost get seasick just looking at the sea," he repeated.

It was only a small transaction, but for both of us it was the right one. A local trucking firm promised to deliver my canoe to Cartagena's Club de Pesca, where I could deck it, seal it water-tight and put it in trim for the oncoming voyage.

My future plans were by now clear. I already knew that I could buy excellent San Blas Indian canoes in Cartagena, which was about 80 miles farther along the azure-blue Caribbean coast from Santa Marta. But since an election was to be held in a few days to elect a new Colombian president, I was in a hurry to be on my way before all transport and road movement stopped for the election fiesta.

# Chapter II

CARTAGENA's Club de Pesca was a haven for Americans, Britons, Australians, as well as the wealthier aristocracy of Colombia's interior. Tourists, of course, were plentiful in the main streets of Cartagena, but they remained at arm's length, outside the club's imposing walls. Sometimes they ventured close enough to photograph the wall's corner battlements, or to ogle the row of rusting cannons still pointed through granite wall-slots at the bay itself. Neutral ground between the residents and ourselves was the club's restaurant, which lay outside the gates, on a harbor knoll. There, we could eat in comfort and yet not be overwhelmed by visitors.

Not that we were recluses. Far from it. It is just that too many landlubbers fail to appreciate that a yachtsman's home, his boat, is his sanctuary. And I was now becoming as attached as a hermit crab to its shell to my tiny Santa Marta canoe. Perhaps, as a bird to its nest would be a more appropriate comparison, for I was certainly no static hermit.

There were a number of yachts fitting-out when I arrived at Cartagena. We all had our own interests. Paul

Johnson was skippering the *Thane* on a delivery job from
Panama to St. Thomas. Dan Lundberg was sailing his steel-
hulled *Passat* with his wife and teen-age son and daughter
on a round-the-world cruise. Dave Beneworth was on his
way to an engineering assignment at St. Croix in the *Pere-
grino.* And Kit Kapp had planned a combination of charter
and Darien exploration in his twin-masted *Windward.*

In such celebrated company I felt somehow out of place,
as though I had entered the Indianapolis "500" with only a
pair of roller skates to my name.

"Ridiculous," said Koronel, who managed the Club de
Pesca's interests. "You have more right to be here than most
behemoth ocean-going yachts."

"I don't even have a sail on my craft as yet," I pointed
out.

"O.K. We will lend you a carpenter, and we will make
you a *bona fide* sailor," he offered.

I thanked him for his offer but explained that I always
liked to work by myself. This is not a matter of egotism; it
is just that I like to know where every nail and every piece
of wood is. Such familiarity breeds confidence, and confidence goes a long way to ensuring success. Koronel was
extremely understanding. He immediately gave me a corner
in the yard where I would not be disturbed and could hammer and saw and slap on paint with as much abandon as I
pleased.

What the others did with their hours in daytime, I do
not know. Doubtless they were all on their respective craft,
for seafaring habits are hard to change, and a spell in a
well-outfitted port always means attending to tasks that
have been neglected at sea or at brief anchor stops. At least
I knew my priority: a deck and cabin, for I needed a place in
which to store tools and supplies if I was to be self-reliant.

In the evenings, however, we would group together or
wander into Cartagena township. Then it would be talk.
Conversations would turn to past trips, and I would learn
that Dan Lundberg had been overhauling blocks and
rigging for most of the day, or that Kit Kapp had been
scrubbing and painting in preparation for a charter group.
Paul Johnson was always busy repairing the wear and tear
of his journey from Panama.

"We had seas as big as walls," he told me, and his
battered skylights and loosened davits certainly seemed to
bear out his horror stories.

Paul and I had a lot in common, although he was certainly a more experienced sailor than myself. In his twenties, he had already sailed the 16-foot *Venus* across the Atlantic and now was "stretching his legs on a larger boat"
before returning to Florida, where he hoped to pick up the
*Venus* and sail to the Bahamas and beyond. I had sailed the
24-foot *Nengo* across the Atlantic in 1961 on much the same
route, and we had many mutual friends.

Perhaps this is where I should write something about
myself; otherwise, I may have to run into all sorts of involved explanations later on.

I have traveled for years, making a fair living writing,
photographing, collecting and trading. When bills have
mounted and my more favorite occupations have let me
down, I have worked at a wide variety of menial jobs.

In March, 1966, when I bought my Santa Marta canoe,
I was 39 years old. Liverpool, England, is my birthplace, but
I have long since adopted Chicago as my home town, or
Chicago had adopted me—whichever way it is, it has been
a mutually pleasant and beneficial liaison.

When I first started traveling, I followed the big money,

in construction sites and bases in the rip-roaring mining towns of Western Australia and Queensland. Then, when I was 22, I decided to open my own photo-finishing studio and dance hall, but I soon learned that as a businessman I was a complete flop. So I meandered through New Zealand and the Polynesian Islands. Later journeys took me through South America and Africa. Europe I have traipsed through half a dozen times, but usually I ignore the more "civilized" routes and look for the more interesting aspects of a place.

Originally, travel-fever was a great excuse to follow the big money, but as it took its grip, I found an ever-increasing urge to travel just for the heck of things. With knowledge and practice I soon started to combine the two. Twelve months travel and twelve months social life is a balance I try (not always successfully) to maintain—a Jekyll and Hyde life, my friends call it.

Usually my travels develop into self-paying projects, although my financial returns are often two to three years behind my outlays; for although stories can be written in a matter of months, it often takes a year or two before they appear on the market.

When I arrived in Cartagena, I had just experienced three exceptionally expensive years. Since 1964 I had made three basic journeys through the Americas. On the first journey I had followed the Pan-American Highway route from New York City to Argentina's Buenos Aires, taking a break en route to make a six-week hike through Panama's Darien with the Cuna Indians—the same people who were later to make my San Blas canoe.

Later, I had followed the rivers by canoe and raft from Argentina's Rio Parana through the Mato Grosso and Amazon to the Orinoco mouth, near Trinidad. And, finally, I had made a journey that was mostly straight jungle-economics during which I had checked into the primitive Amazon Indians' method of treating leishmaniasis (an ulcer common to South America's jungles) in southern Colombia.

The journeys had cost a lot of money and returned little. For example, I had been trying to sell a book called *Secrets of the Medicine Men,* which gave an account of my South American travels, but to no avail. Thus, I had had to work through most of the previous summer and winter repairing my bank balance.

Fortunately, the traveler is never restricted to one form of work. For example, one interesting by-product of my recent South American journeys was that Dr. Donald Collier, Chief Curator of Chicago's Field Museum, had suggested I be on the lookout for a dugout canoe. Should I find a good specimen, Dr. Collier said, there was a good chance that the museum would buy it for display and to complete its already extensive South American collection.

This was certainly satisfactory for both of us, for on canoes I count myself an expert. I have spilled from the unbalanced torched dugouts of the Australian Aborigines, clung to narrow dart-like praus in the Borneo rapids, luxuriated in the trim catamarans of Polynesia and raced smartly in the finely crafted Soon Kosi River canoes of Nepal. Over the years I have developed a *feel* that is almost second nature. I can never for the life of me understand why a man shopping for a car will kick the tires of a vehicle he fancies, and yet I have thumped the hulls of a thousand canoes and said, "Now *there* is a fine craft," or, "This is a lemon."

Before buying my new canoe, I had made a six weeks' journey around some Amazon tributaries, collecting blowguns, bark blankets, amulets and such things. But subconsciously I suspected that this year was going to be associated with canoes and canoe-travel. I had even made a list of some of the craft that I could purchase. The Mariposa canoe of the Upper Orinoco would have looked elegant, its upswept bow and stern dramatizing a dignified museum setting. The sturdy fundamentals of the Cascus, Santa Rens, Desaladors or Ovadas canoes were impressive. The 60-foot-long Bongos of Venezuela's Pioroa tribe would be fine—if you had enough paddlers. In fact, all of these craft would have been splendid. The main difficulty would have been transportation between South America's interior and Chicago.

And thus one returns to my present journey. I would canoe to Chicago. But, meantime, I would use the various useful trades—carpentry, painting and general nailsman-ship—that I had acquired along my travels. They had served me well before; they could again.

Almost to the last minute, I was not sure which route to take to the Mississippi mouth. The Caribbean section was the difficulty. I dickered between going "straight-down-the-middle," from Cartagena to the Yucatan Straits, and following the mainland coast, in a giant arc as far as the Yucatan headland.

I remember talking it over with Paul Johnson, over a tall, ice-cold beer.

"It's a long journey if I don't make the direct run," I explained to him.

"But the heavy surf is going to cost you a lot of busy hours and energy. As well as that, you'll be risking your craft on the rocks," Paul pointed out logically.

"Of course, you are the skipper," Paul went on, "but you had best guess right first time. You cannot make second guesses at sea."

Though I dithered, I came slowly to realize that Paul

was right. And I came to my decision none too soon. It was important I know what my route would be before I laid my canoes together, for there is always more strain near the inland waters, and more catamarans come to grief by yawing between stormy channels than by rolling smoothly over deep ocean waves.

Together, Paul and I went over the Pilot Charts— United States Naval Oceanographic maps marked incongruously *"NOT TO BE USED FOR NAVIGATIONAL PURPOSES"*—for they are the finest yacht maps I know. Issued monthly, they give a statistical estimation of the direction and speed of the winds and currents.

Everything certainly seemed in my favor for a good crossing. Ice-cold beer bottles emptied as Paul and I made routes and calculations on the charts' surfaces. And if the routes looked a little erratic, and we had headaches the next morning, we both admitted we had learned a lot the previous night.

"Don't stay near the coast, and don't drink that terrible *Caribe* beer," Paul advised.

I was not in a position to argue. And in that vein I think I should set down a couple of rules, which I had made a few years before, that I think typified my attitude to the forthcoming voyage, because they are my "safeguards." My first principle at sea is: *if a boat does not sink, then you cannot drown—provided you use a lifeline.*

In this case, my boat was to be hollowed trunks of trees, and there was no danger of their sinking. Even if the canoes split apart, and I was swamped for a month, there would still be no danger. True, a swamped boat is not very comfortable. But comfort sometimes has to be a secondary thing where safety is concerned. I have floated on balsa rafts along the South American coast and been wet for days on end, and

I know that being soaked continually by salt water does no more harm than skin-diving. (Incidentally, I might add that balsa rafts are seldom made of balsa wood. *Balsa* merely is the Spanish for "raft," and normal rafts are of such hardwood as the same caracoli as my own Santa Marta canoe.)

My second rule is: *if you have enough food aboard, then you will not go hungry or thirsty.* Once, however, I forgot a can opener on a journey to the French River in Canada, but that only goes to prove that every rule has an exception.

As I made lists of all the stores I would need for a Caribbean crossing, I kept to the same rules, which really amount to a general principle: *that no journey is safe unless every reasonable precaution is taken.*

My Santa Marta canoe had been scrubbed down with a stiff-bristled scrub-brush, to check on the possibility of flaws or hidden knot-holes. In fact, what had originally been a tiny section of the Club de Pesca work yard now was the size of half a tennis court, and a sawbench and carpenter's table had been filched to make my work easier. Koronel, instead of being in despair that I was commandeering his equipment, was actually encouraging me. He even suggested that I fence it off, for visitors were beginning to prowl around, to view the strange sight of a primitive canoe being transformed into a fire-engine-red sea-going boat.

Red seemed to be an appropriate color for the craft. Red and black. Ethnological colors from way back before stone-age times. A further advantage of this color scheme was that I needed to buy only two different paints and two paint brushes. I called the paint fire-engine-red, but in actual practice, the name on the tin was *Chino Rojo,* Chinese Red. And it was not long before my craft was being dubbed *The Chinese Navy,* and I the Admiral.

"How is the Admiral of the Chinese Navy?" Koronel used to greet me.

I would give him a flip-finger salute and say, "Operation's going according to plan, Colonel."

Koronel actually was Koronel's name; it had nothing to do with military rank. But the tourists did not know this, and word got around that I was being given a military escort on my "grand operation."

Work swung along at a fast rate—faster than I had anticipated—and the hull length was soon completely sealed. Even I was impressed with the obvious strength and water-tightness of the joins. Not even the most powerful of hurricanes would be able to drive water through the solid, inch-thick decking or to budge the two-inch nails. The tarred and oakum-caulked planks were so firmly sealed they would have done credit to a submarine.

*If all reasonable precautions are not taken, then the journey is not valid* was the adage I was keeping to. That may sound too serious (though it was not). Perhaps "Dry the wood, pour on hot tar and never the two shall leak" is more appropriate.

My muscles ached with the number of nails I had banged in and the pails of tar I had hefted. Nails were bought in five-pound sacks, and the number I used soon escaped my memory. Tar was cheap, no more than five dollars a hundred pounds, and I had no hesitation about ladling it on where any potential weakness showed.

My yachting friends were horrified. "You are sabotaging the good work of a hundred years of nautical science," they said sorrowfully.

I would leer, and drive in another iron nail, and pour another ladle of asphalt, and let them cough and choke as the acrid fumes wafted up their noses. Still, I am sure that the tears they had in their eyes were not solely caused by the bitter smoke of the boiling tar.

Slowly, a gallery began to collect on the other side of the rails. Many of its members were naval officers, but first they changed into mufti to save themselves the embarrassment of being recognized near my workshop.

Even the Harbor Master came over, and his conversation was very much to the point.

"Are you sure you are going to sail?"

"I am quite sure."

"Are you sure you do not want to change your mind?"

"Yes."

"Humph," he snorted. "Well, I guess there is no reason to stop you."

Election Day sneaked up on me faster than I had expected. As usual, I prowled around with a sack over my right shoulder, shifty eyes darting into windows as I passed, always searching for something which might have some use in my compact cabin. It seemed the right way to go about things when cash was still such a problem. But on that day I had not gone far before suspicious glances were aimed at me as I wandered through the crowd-thronged streets in work clothes, in search of yet another five-pound sack of nails. I thought it all absurd. Why the fuss? Bars were closed, and traffic was almost at a standstill. But nothing bothered me much—at first. Getting nails cheaply is a serious business! In fact, I was so preoccupied that I did not realize that armed troops stood guard at the major street corners and, as I saw later, over the ballot boxes in the center thoroughfares of the city.

Often during past elections, ballot boxes had been stuffed with incendiary devices. This time, however, before the voters were allowed to step forward and vote for their candidate, they were frisked to make sure they had nothing more lethal than ballot sheets about their persons. Foreign correspondents, police and military searched for statistics, drama or electoral abuse—according to their wont. Armored trucks and riot squads made their presence known at all the major intersections. Once more the forts of Cartagena became important, for these were natural polling stations. Me? Well, I just hammered on the door of my favorite *ferretéria* store and received a fresh sack of two-inch nails.

"Caramba! We even have tourists to contend with," ejaculated a guard, as he frisked me of my nails and pliers. After this I stayed clear of Cartagena city walls and made my way back to my dugout hull.

But once having been through the rigmarole, I took more interest in the election. Since peace had been established in 1952 after four years of bloody civil war, it has been accepted national policy to alternate electoral winners between the Liberals and the Conservatives. This year it was expected that Carlos Lleras, an economics expert, would be the winner.

With nothing better to do, I added the final touches to my Santa Marta canoe: the deck house and cabin, a low affair that barely allowed me head clearance when I sat. I didn't much care. I still thought that I was going only to Chicago, and that the journey would take 90 days at the maximum. Still, to make the cabin more livable, I built in shallow shelves to hold my shaving gear, eating utensils, notebooks, films and such luxury items as sunglasses and chinaware—plebeian maybe, but practical.

Instead of my usual cedar-planking, I invested in half-inch sea-ply. This allowed me to have a sloped roof, thus combining strength with the utility of faster draining. Even the finest of flawless woods was ridiculously cheap in jungle-rich Colombia, and sea-ply, at $10 a sheet, was a definite luxury.

The cabin done, I could have moved bodily into my finished hull. And when I examined the situation, I found an unexpected bonus. While testing the hull for height, I discovered that I had three inches' clearance, enough to give me room for a mattress, which would soften the hard dugout deck. And yet I was in no hurry to move into my cramped, if adequate, new quarters, especially since alternative accommodations were still available.

While I had been working on the hull, I had been living on Paul's *Thane*, along with Clayton, Larry and Brian—three of the other crew members—and I had become accustomed to company. Our chores had been equally divided, with one doing the cooking, another the tidying, and the third keeping the deck space and dock moorings spick-and-span; Paul and I bought most of the day-to-day stores when we made our daily forays into town. With such an easy life, it was no wonder I was reluctant to move into my own hull immediately, and Paul suggested I stay aboard the *Thane* until he left.

"Your cabin's no larger than a dinghy," he said.

That may have been true, but it was a well-designed dinghy. "We have both crossed the Atlantic in smaller craft than mine," I mentioned, feeling I should put up some show.

"That is no reason to make yourself more uncomfortable than necessary."

I had no intention of arguing further.

Two girls—Louise and a friend—shared a cabin launch

just along the quay from us. They were both happily married, so there were no shenanigans, and they were part of the communal group. There was no shortage of girls downtown—less than half-a-dozen blocks away—if we wanted to go fooling around.

I had been so preoccupied with trying to bring my craft in order that I had completely ignored everything else.

"You have never seen the pretty beaches of Boca Chica," Louise accused me. "And all you do all day is stick your nose into your pokey canoe. You never even see what is going on around you."

She was right, and I began to grow discontented. Also, although I did not tell Louise this, I wanted to go to Boca Chica to buy another canoe, for Boca Chica is where most of the best San Blas canoes are, and it was a San Blas canoe I needed for an outrigger to balance my hull and stabilize my catamaran. In fact, the decision was easily made.

"O.K.," I said. "Let's go to Boca Chica as soon as we can."

"You've never seen the city either," Louise kept on, "or our beautiful cathedral and parks."

"Honestly, Louise," I defended myself, "I would just love to go to all these places, but I must get my boat made and be on my way before the hurricane season starts and the weather becomes too dangerous to sail."

I was exaggerating, for sailing and commerce do not stop because of the hurricane season, and I had faith I would build my craft to ride out any storms. But I was keen to be on my way without too much delay, for Chicago was 3,190 miles away, and it would take me the best part of summer to sail across the Caribbean and the Gulf and motor up the river.

I had bought my Santa Marta canoe on March 17, and it was now early April. My plans called for me to finish my craft by May 1—45 days from start to finish, less than a month and a half.

"You yachtsmen are all the same," Louise said, miffed. "Always too busy to do anything else."

Paul came to my rescue. "Let's make a date to go on the *Thane* to Boca Chica next Sunday," he suggested.

The crisis was over.

Looking back on it now, I can see how very lucky I was in everything in Cartagena. The canoes I bought were fine and reasonably priced. And everything happened at the right time to fit nicely into my tight schedule, even allowing me time to think. Meanwhile, however, Sunday was only a few days off and I had no shortage of work to do, for there were many tiny details to take care of, such as buying stores and provisions and checking the different designs I could use for sail and rigging. And then, of course, there still was the matter of my second canoe.

When I had first arrived in Cartagena, I had made the usual tour of the waterfront and had been appalled at the poor quality of the canoes there. Almost all had had their stern sections sawn off and outboard motor fittings attached, and their insides were blackened with oil and grease—the result of spillage from the auxiliary gasoline tanks and taking care of the motors.

"I had heard that they have fine canoes around here," I had complained. "And all I can see is junk."

"These are fine canoes, senor," the fisherman had maintained, draping fishing nets over inch-wide cracks and surreptitiously hammering in six-inch nails to prevent the stern pieces from wobbling. As word passed around that I was on the lookout for a canoe, wonderful things were offered to me, all of which ranged in decay and age, or so it seemed, back to pre-Columbian days.

"Now here is a fine canoe," one harbor rogue declared, showing me to a rolled-over wreck that the locals used as a waterfront seat and card table.

"It may not be a fine canoe, but it certainly looks interesting," I said, as I wondered what I would find underneath when I turned it over.

Four of us spread along the canoe's length, worked our fingers under the rim and heaved it right-side-up. Crabs ran in all directions, and a small black rat blinked its eyes as the unexpected daylight lit its dry-driftwood nest. The canoe rolled all the way over, and seldom have I seen a more rot-encased hull.

"It just needs cleaning a little, senor," my hopeful salesman doubtfully assured me.

"It is sacrilege to disturb such ancient monuments," I murmured and made my way back to the marketplace.

I made the harbor part of my daily tour. Everything was called "a fine canoe, and cheap." "*Mucho fino, y barato.*" Such was the description I heard of everything on the waterfront. Later I was to learn that the San Blas islanders encouraged this state of affairs. "Cartagena has no need for deep-water craft, except for fishing," I was told. And the San Blas canoes were so superior in choppy deep water that all the best canoes were grabbed by the active fishing community. And most of these fishermen were based in Boca Chica, 12 miles down-harbor. Cartagena city took the castoffs, and the castoffs were in poor condition.

"Is there any chance of importing a San Blas canoe direct, from the islands?" I asked Captain Gomez, a coastal

copra trader who ran his twin-masted schooner toward the
Panama coast every two weeks.

"Not a chance," he said. "Taxes and freight charges
play havoc with the prices, and, in any case, it could take
months to find you one."

Most canoes are smuggled in. The Rosario Islands are
a favorite base, as are the mutually convenient fishing
grounds further west, just off the unpatrolled Colombian
coast. The smuggling is a profitable business for all concerned. Since there were no taxes to be paid, by buyer or
seller, both could make better bargains. More important,
the red tape necessary to register the sale and importing is
all but eliminated, and middleman profits also are bypassed.

"You will have no difficulty at all buying all the canoes
you need in Boca Chica," Captain Gomez assured me.

Sunday came, a glorious day: 65 degrees, little wind,
the harbor glass-smooth.

"Not much good for sailing," Paul grumbled.

"Fine. Let's use the motor," said Louise, and I echoed
her sentiments. I would be doing enough sailing on my own
in a few weeks' time.

We weighed anchor and headed down-bay at six knots.
On our starboard were the Boca Grande suburbs—a richer
section of the town, trim and shining with white houses and
patio walls mixed with the verdant green of domesticated
tree-lined streets. The Caribe Hotel stood out in gaudy
splendor at the cape head. Tiny swimming pools and kiosks
lined the waterfront. A microcosm of suburban life, Boca
Grande seemed to offer more a suggestion of the leisure its
inhabitants wanted than of the leisure they had.

Cartagena Bay is a shallow bay, with shifting sandbanks

and narrow channels. Even Paul had become stuck as he had attempted to negotiate the channel to the Club de Pesca when he had first arrived.

"Nine feet is just too much draught to sail through eight and a half feet of water," Paul had reasoned logically while waiting for the tide to rise—to escape from the embarrassment of being aground in view of everyone in the harbor.

This time the tide was high, and we passed the shallows easily.

Most of the shore which is not built-up, or under cultivation, is lined with mangrove. There are many beaches the 15-mile length of the harbor, but not many of these have shade trees. And consequently Boca Chica, a delightful beach, is popular. Already half a dozen power cruisers and yachts were there when we arrived, and we anchored a quarter-mile from shore, giving ourselves plenty of room to swing on the anchor. Fifteen feet of sparkling water was under our keel as we hailed a passing fisherman, who earned a fair day's cash each Sunday ferrying visitors to the shore and back.

One of the crew stayed aboard, and the rest of us assembled our gear. Paul and the other crew members went for a swim; I cornered Louise, and we set off to reconnoiter the far-off fishing village, which nestled in the recessed arm of a shallow bay about a half-mile away.

Even a cursory glance told me I was in the right place. Canoes were everywhere. Tippy two-passenger canoes. Sailing auxiliary-motor canoes, with high lee-boards to ward off the wake. Fishing canoes, stale with fish smells and packed to the brim with fishing nets and floats. Forty-foot-long water-carriers (most fresh water is brought in by the tank-load from mainland fresh-water wells). The colors were just as spectacular, and again I was impressed how even muddy-blacks or dingy-grays, colors of mourning in our own cold countries, seemed to glitter and gleam in the tropic sun. We kicked through the fine sand with our bare toes, or trailed along the shallow water if we hit a stony patch. Black-winged seagulls wheeled overhead, scavenging for fish, and lizards scampered in the nearby bushes.

"The Club de Pesca should be here," Louise said.

"Then I would never get any work done," I mused.

The fishing village was not tidy by any standards. But then fishing villages seldom are. Houses stood festooned with empty turtle shells, garden lots littered with parts of discarded motors and cables. Sailfish fins tacked against the walls. Coconuts drying in the sun—for the copra or the meat. Shellfish heaps, where chowders had been made. A broken hull here. A discarded pair of oars, the family wash strung on a line between them. Empty cans. Bottles. There was even a heavy electric sewing machine. How it worked I would not know, for we could see no sign of electrical cables. Such was Boca Chica.

Sunday was a day of rest, and most of the town's varied population were in their church clothes. Many of them were just coming back from church, a small whitewashed concrete building, behind the town's waterfront hut-line.

Louise and I made the round of the canoes, pausing at each long enough for the locals to realize that we were seriously looking for a craft but not long enough for them to know which type of craft we had in mind. Bare-bottomed children and lean-ribbed dogs ran around us by the hundreds. Some fishermen were already back in work clothes and sat in the shade of their sails mending nets, and their wives sat under the huts' eaves and gutted fish in buckets of salt water. They did not look at us directly, but we knew that they had their eyes and ears trained our way.

I would have been fair game if I had ventured here by myself, for nothing brings out the mercenary instincts of a fisherman easier than a prospective boat-buyer. But Louise, a godsend, dug out an impressive sneer and said none of the canoes were fit for firewood. I kicked the first hull to hear its sound, but than I realized I was in bare feet and contented myself thereafter with knocking the hulls with my knuckles, or with hitting them with a piece of driftwood if I needed more resonance. Owners drifted across to assess the performance. I had made my choice, though we still had the sellers bluffed.

"This is a fast craft for racing, senor," a leading fisherman said.

"Too narrow, and the tree was twisted," I pointed out.

We eliminated the vessels one by one, while I ascertained what the prices were.

"This will carry cargo for many years more."

"This is a lucky canoe. I caught more fishes than anyone else in the village last year."

"A fine canoe. And I wouldn't sell it, except it belongs to my wife's widowed sister."

"Cheap. And you can trail it behind your yacht." The pitches were wonderful.

"I just want a small canoe to paddle around the harbor," I countered.

Eventually we came alongside the craft I wanted, a pretty canoe, although a little heavy by San Blas standards. There was a place for the mast, but the seat-hole showed sharp splinters. Obviously none had been steeped. The black hull and green-and-yellow bands seemed to fit nicely

to its shape. "Twenty-two-foot long. Three-foot-six wide,"
I noted—a perfect match for my Santa Marta hull.

I had bartered for the other craft, now I swung around
to this.

"Two thousand pesos," said the stump-armed man at
my side.

It was worth maybe 1,200, and I knew it. "One thousand
pesos," I bargained. "And I am robbed at that price."

He grinned as though I had made a joke.

I thought I would be serious, and honest. "It is worth
1,200 maximum." I told him.

He swore he would not sell it for a centavo less than
1,800, and we finally made a deal at 1,600 pesos.

"Eighty-eight dollars," I mused. Not a bad price at all.
I was now the proud owner of a second canoe. Juan Marino
wagged his handless stump, showing me he could not write
or sign a receipt. But we trooped into his fishing hut, and on
his soap-crate living-room table a friend made a bill of sale.

It was a solemn and serious ceremony.

One-handed fishermen are all too common along the
Caribbean coast. Dynamiting fish is illegal—Colombia
banned it years ago, not from any moral standpoint, but
purely because it is uneconomical. Unfortunately, the
industry is still a major source of income with small-boat
fishermen, especially when they are alone in a large school
of fish or if the fish are not biting. Half a stick of dynamite
in a stone-weighted can or bottle will stop everything for
20 feet around. The concussion lasts long enough for a
fisherman to catch 15 to 20 fish with a minimum of effort.
Unfortunately, the explosion also has a tendency to wreck
the fishes' swimming bladders and fully 90 percent are
liable to sink to the bottom, unseen and uncollected. Fishermen around the area the next few days will find the remain-

ing fish spooked away, and in time a whole fishing ground can be destroyed.

Juan had been even more unfortunate than most. Sharks have now learned to associate the sound of dynamite explosions with food. At first they were frightened away by the explosion's sound; now an explosion is liable to bring them from more than a mile away.

Usually there is no danger to anyone in a boat from even the most ferocious of sharks. But Juan had grabbed at one too many stunned fishes at the wrong time. As he had grabbed, a shark had zoomed up from beneath the canoe's shade.

"We both grabbed for the same fish at the same time," said Juan ruefully, as he wagged his handless stump.

Business concluded, Louise and I wandered back to the beach again. Paul and the crew lay sprawled on the yellow sand, and since Juan had promised to paddle the canoe over to the *Thane*, the afternoon was free.

I could breathe easier now. I was sure I had chosen two of the best dugouts, from two of the best canoe-types. The predecessors had been plying the waters for thousands of years. Doubtless canoes smaller than mine had crossed oceans before, often being dismasted or caught in contrary storms. The little crossing of the Caribbean no longer worried me.

The San Blas was "pure," in the ethnological sense, and would be perfect for the Field Museum. My old Santa Marta canoe was a hybrid, for it had been carved by people of mixed Indian-Negro blood—Zambos they are called: "Not either," say the purists. "A little bit of both," is my opinion.

By a quirk of circumstances, this "little bit of both" was

to become most appropriate; for it was to take a "pure" San Blas canoe as an outrigger to Chicago and later to bring a "pure" Wolof canoe back from Africa.

"Now is your time to see the castle," Louise reminded me. And, indeed, Cartagenans have every reason to be proud of their colorful past. In most Spanish-speaking countries foreign naval heroes are usually regarded as little more than pirates, and this applies especially to English admirals. In Cartagena, Sir Francis Drake, Sir Walter Raleigh, Grenville and Vernon head the list of renegades, and another was Lawrence Washington, half-brother to George Washington and an officer in Vernon's fleet.

Local history has always intrigued me, and after a light lunch, Louise and I started off to the Boca Chica castle grounds. A few links of heavy chain still lay around. Once they had been buoyed across the harbor to combat furtive hostile entrance, in much the same way that cable nets are presently strewn across our own harbors to fend-off enemy submarines in wartime. In fact, Boca Chica had once been a self-dependent settlement, established to guard the point and repel or delay the ceaseless adventurers and raiders, for Cartagena, almost from its foundation in the early 1500's, had been envied for its wealth. From almost every angle along the harbor's length one can see a castle or fortified strongpoint.

Even in those far-off days, the San Blas canoes (or similar types) were kept at hand, to dart into combat with fire arrows and small-bore cannon. But the Spanish garrison-soldier never felt at home in the water, and no successes—to my knowledge—were recorded. In any case, times change. And the purpose of my San Blas canoe, now bobbing along behind us as we motored homeward, was to be different. And, to Louise, its destiny needed to be marked.

"We must have a proper launching party soon," she said.

I looked doubtfully at the tiny San Blas canoe trailing in our wake. It hardly looked large enough to warrant such an honor.

"Size is just a matter of relativity," said Paul, answering my thoughts. He also considered we should have a celebration.

I thought it over.

"A small launching party," I agreed.

The pace quickened. My finished craft was taking shape, and a very satisfactory one it was. The decks of both the original canoes were now covered and sealed. The resin and tar and smell of freshly sawn wood gave my completed hulls a pleasant tang. I borrowed a trick from my car-tire-kicking friends, and I hammered on the hull until it boomed like a drum, and over tinny-weak sounds I would hammer on another support or ladle more tar.

Every day the local fishermen peered through the club railings, their crinkled faces wise and puzzled, and they would tap their suntanned forehead and murmur, "*El señor entende.*" At least, their confidence helped.

Dry rot had shown up in the San Blas canoe, and I had been a trifle concerned as I uncovered two large sections, one nearly a foot long. You simply cannot gamble on such weak places holding out at sea, so I cut the rot-weakened parts back to live wood and replaced the sections with blocks and wedges. Here again, tar was the main time-saver, and the hull never gave me trouble again.

So far I had not chosen a name, nor had a stage been reached when a name seemed suitable. Frankly, my mind was on different matters, for I was still making daily trips to town or the local market for necessary items, and I was delving into a different and unknown vocabulary: *algoynas, cadena, tornillos et tuercas, clavos, pintura, brea.* My Spanish expanded as I asked for eye-bolts, chain, nuts and bolts, nails, paint, tar and hundreds of other items. The naval commissary was opened to me, should I wish to buy anything from their stores at duty-free prices. But most of their supplies were for large ocean-going ships, and one of their anchors would have been heavy enough to sink me.

Chain was one of the most difficult things to buy. The commissary had chain by the roomful, but this again was deep-sea chain. Some individual links weighed as much as twenty-two pounds; my whole anchor only weighed five pounds. For some reason all of the hardware stores also were out of chain, and I had had to send to Barranquilla for a supply.

The two hulls were now afloat, held together by a sturdy X-shaped platform. Experimenting is a lot of fun, and I doubt if I would travel if everything consistently went as routine. My present craft was a perfect excuse to indulge in numerous pet construction theories.

The frame that held the canoes together was of *abarco* wood, a beautiful straight-grained timber, as strong as oak and as supple as yew. Canvas-covered chain links held the craft together firmly, tightened with heavy eye-bolts set in the main frame while the canoes were high and dry.

Two advantages of this construction were that ethnologically the canoes were in the same condition as when I bought them, and that no holes through the hulls meant no place for leaks. The only leeway I allowed myself was the six holes I drilled through the solid stern-post to support the rudder housing and they could be plugged later.

Rubber gaskets placed between each canoe deck and

the frame helped to prevent slippage. When the finished craft was put in the water, the canoe-hulls swelled, and I could hear the chains grind as they clenched into place. Even the hurricane I encountered in the Caribbean did not budge them.

The masts and spars were palo amarillo, a wonderfully hard wood, popular all along the Colombian coast for the local fishing vessels. As saplings they cost me 28 pesos, or $1.40, and the professional yachtsmen grimaced as I cut them down to size on my solid deck.

"This craft can go anywhere in the world," I told my disbelievers, as I swept bark, twigs and leaves into the water.

For the rigging, instead of steel cable, I used heavy wood-baling wire, the kind they use to keep telephone poles steady. I was pretty sure that if it would keep telephone poles aloft, it was certainly capable of keeping my masts firm. An equally important point was the fact that it only cost 60 cents to rig the boat completely with the wire, and cash was getting short.

Sails would be 200 square feet of awning canvas, for I still thought I was making a one-way trip to Chicago only. If I had known the journey would be extended to cover the Atlantic, then I would have used a minimum of 400 square feet, so that I could aim closer into the wind.

I stood back to examine my handiwork, and a light hand tapped me on my shoulder.

"We've arranged a launching party," Louise said.

A grinning Paul, bottle in his hand, let his eye wander to where Louise was supposed to smash it over my bow.

"I haven't got a name for it yet," I objected. "Besides, no one is going to smash any sticky bottle over my hull until the paint is dry."

"All sea-going boats have bottles smashed over them,"
Louise said.

"Not mine," I repeated. "Besides, I'm darned if I will
put to sea with bits of glass stuck all over the canvas."

"Let's go back to the launch and drink it then," suggested Louise.

It was the best idea I had heard that day. It was late in
the afternoon, and there was little sense in returning to
work. Louise suggested we go away and get dressed and come
back later for evening dinner.

Paul had had a telegram from his yacht's owner that the
yacht was wanted in Miami, and he intended to sail in a
couple of days, when a few galley parts out for repair were
returned. My own craft was now almost completed, and I
could live aboard in relative comfort.

"I'll be sorry to leave this port," Paul said, and I could
see what he meant. It hardly seemed that I had been here less
than a month, so much had been done and time had gone so
fast.

I set May 1 as the date for my test sail, to check how the
vessel steered. I had designed the sails and masts in such a
way that I should be self-steering on almost every course,
and it would be easier to balance the craft in the sheltered
harbor than in the turbulent sea.

While we dressed, Paul told me of some of the trips he
had made around the Scottish coast and the European Lowland countries.

"Now *that* is tough sailing," said Paul, "with the wind
coming from all directions, and cold enough to make a
polar bear freeze."

I doubt if I would ever have learned to sail if I had had
to rely on that type of weather. My initial sailing had been

done on the *Nengo*, a 24-foot Norwegian double-ender, five years earlier. I could not sail when I had first started the journey, and I had learned on the way across the Atlantic in the cooperative trade winds.

I am usually a plodder. Speed seldom interests me much. At least speed does not interest me if it brings along discomfort at the same time, and I am always nervous on a yacht if it is speeding along at 12–15 knots, keeling over at 45 degrees, or at some such uncomfortable angle.

Paul and I took along a six-pack of beer, and Louise and her friend were cooking a fine-smelling dinner as we went aboard her launch. White tablecloth, red wine, a stereo playing music. This was to be a going-away party for Louise also, for she had to return to Bogota the following morning.

The unexpected happened early.

Louise came swooshing in with a platter of fish, and the four of us sat down to dine in comfort. I asked casually what the fish was.

"*Sierra*," said Louise.

"I thought *Sierra* meant mountain?" I queried.

"It does," said Louise. "But *Sierra* also means a saw made for cutting wood."

She went on to explain: It is the serrated mountain ridge that is properly called *Sierra*. The same teeth-like serrations are on a hand saw. On the back of the mackerel is a series of fins, the dorsal fins, with the same type of serration. And a local colloquialism for mackerel is *Sierra*.

In much the same manner, the giant 400-pound horse-mackerel is known as *caballo*, or horse.

I thought it over. A passing American tourist had passed my craft and said, "*Holy Mackerel! What is that!*" It somehow seemed appropriate. *SIERRA SAGRADA. HOLY MACKEREL!*

I had a name for my boat.

"*Sierra Sagrada*," we toasted.

Later, in the French ports of Canada and St. Pierre, the locals took to calling it *Sacre Maquereau*—which I immediately recognized as a Gallic version of *Holy Mackerel*. What I did not learn for several days is that *maquereau* is Paris-slang known the Gallic-world over. It means *gigolo*. The French had given my boat's name their own translation. *Holy Gigolo*, they called it. But even this was not inappropriate. For the *Sierra Sagrada* cost me every penny I had and kept me flat-broke for a long time to come.

The Club de Pesca did not seem the same with Paul and Louise gone. My boat was now afloat, adorned with the fresh nameplate *Sierra Sagrada*, painted red on a white background. The sails had been fitted, and all that remained was to collect the few final fresh provisions.

"Why don't you move into the *Thane*'s old position?" Koronel offered.

This suited me fine. My sails were too small to try any fancy sailing between the banks of craft in the rear channel's crowded pathway, and catamarans are notoriously difficult to sail at slow speeds.

"I will only be a few days," I promised, for I did not want to take the premium space in the Club de Pesca's harbor.

My plan was to tack across to Boca Grande, then follow Tierra Bomba, or Fire Island, until I was half-way along Cartagena's harbor. Then I would return along the far bank, on the morning breezes the following day. Such a trip would test the sails out at all angles.

I bought supplies for the complete voyage and loaded them carefully so that the weight trim would not need to be altered. Some 60 pounds of varied meats, fruits, soups, with my favorite old standby of spaghetti and beans made up the bulk of the commissary. Fresh fruit and bread supplies I would collect when I returned after the try-out.

A useful wind dominates Cartagena harbor. In the early morning the wind blows from the west; later in the day it changes direction, coming from the east. It is like going downhill all the way. It was late afternoon when Koronel cast my lines clear, and I veered into the midstream for the *Sierra Sagrada*'s maiden journey. I did not move fast— about three knots I estimated—but that was satisfactory. All I wanted to do was to deliver the canoes. Speed was of secondary importance.

"He'll never make it to the other side," I heard someone remark. Clearly, since the opposite bank was less than a mile away, they hadn't too much faith in my design or workmanship.

My aim was to stay at Boca Chica overnight, but my steering was less vigorous than I had anticipated, and the winds took me further downstream than I had planned. Rather than be pushed down harbor as far as Boca Chica, I set course for the southern bank and hove-to at about seven-thirty, just as it was getting dark.

A problem showed itself with the rudder. I had not sailed catamarans before and therefore had not realized the large surface area needed to get a grip. My only previous sailing had been on the *Nengo*, which was so skittish that it would almost turn around on a dime.

Sleeping out for the first night at anchor, I checked a few simple calculations that should allow the *Sierra Sagrada* to handle better. It was satisfactory to note that neither of my hulls suffered from even the slightest leak, and apart from the drift, the balanced sails held their course on any position I chose. Obviously the few adjustments I would need to make would not delay me long.

Rather than return the next morning, I unhooked the rudder and tacked extension pieces along the rear edge and on the lower sections. The surface area was at least doubled, and even while anchored in the strong tideflats I could feel the extra area take grip. While at anchor, I also secured the standing rigging more securely, clamping the trailing rigging-ends low on the mast to prevent tangling. All told, I was immensely pleased with the whole rig. It was a shame the sails were not larger, but I had no intention of changing them now.

One can always find a host of small things to do on boats, and I spent the morning restowing food and trimming the edges off a foam-rubber mattress, trying to make the *Sierra Sagrada* as shipshape as possible.

This was the first complete day I had had to myself for a month, and it was so late in the afternoon when I had finished that I decided to delay my start twenty-four hours. Consequently I was a day overdue when I arrived back at the Club de Pesca, and I was received with a warm reception. News was short in the newspaper business: the election had come and gone, and Lleras had been elected. It had been a peaceful affair with total casualties over the whole country amounting to no more than a handful killed and a few score wounded. The police were back to revolvers only, and the troops were hidden once more in their barren camps in the city's outskirts.

An old problem, however, had arisen in Cartagena, and I shared one of the middle pages of the local paper with the rodent problem. It seemed that the previous year a series of heavy rains had driven the city's rodent population from their underground burrows to the select community of a newly built residential district. Many cities would have accepted this development equably, but not Cartagena, a city of pride. A committee was formed to combat the invasion. Poison-bait was laid across the city in a carefully scheduled counter-attack. Unfortunately, the plan went wrong. The rats flourished, and the bait was hungrily devoured by the city's army of underfed stray cats. The final results were that the city had as many rats as ever and too few cats to keep them under control, and the value of cats became inflated. Warehouses and stores paid premium prices for any kittens, toms or females that could be collected.

With such a lively market stray cats and pedigreed—everything was included—were all literally pounced upon. No cat was safe. Cats were even kidnapped from the most select suburbs. Eventually, nature in her own proliferant way, returned the balance. But, meanwhile, "cat-napping" abounded.

The best laid plans of mice and men . . .

# Chapter III

GREEN seas slapped into clouds of fine spray as I hit the rolling incoming waves of the Caribbean. The provisioned *Sierra Sagrada* plowed forward as trim and tidy as a seagull. Dan Lundberg, Jeff Benniworth and the Club de Pesca staff had given me a noisy send-off, and there was no turning back. Koronel had thrown me the last mooring rope and yelled a boisterous: "*Bon voyage.*"

A friendly wind carried me through the Boca Grande gap, and I kept to the channel center. Boca Chica is the usual entrance for deep-sea craft. But this would have entailed a six-mile detour, and I preferred the less traveled entrance instead.

Originally access to Cartagena had been available by two *bocas: Boca Grande*, adjacent to the town, and *Boca Chica*, where Fort San Fernando lay. But after Admiral Vernon's abortive raid, the town's defenders had built a wall three feet under the water's surface as a defense measure. One of the world's marvels in planning ingenuity and construction, if need be, the wall could serve the same service

39

today: allowing nonaggressive coastal-traders to pass, but keeping hostile warships at bay.

Time and waves have eroded the top peak off the wall, and the *Sierra Sagrada* and I passed through into the open sea with ease. From the shore the roar of busy evening street traffic became muted as I eased myself seaward; the bustling cars began to look like tiny clockwork toys, remote from reality.

Radio Cartagena was saying that the weather for the following 24 hours would be favorable, and I had no reason to doubt it. All told, I had that smug feeling of a job well done. Lively music was playing, and I ate part of the half-chicken that the Club de Pesca had given me before I left.

The sky faded as the sun set, and a canopy of stars took over. Lights flickered on one by one on the shoreline. Each one could be individually distinguished at first, but they slowly faded into a night-glow as I moved further out and Cartagena darkened into a faint silhouette behind the sea-cliffs.

I stayed at the tiller until past midnight, aiming into the black night and gaining as much distance from the shore as possible. To my mind the only certain danger near shore is that of running into shoals or rocks of the coast itself. And downwind of the *Sierra Sagrada* lay a group of islands called the Rosarios, but known to sailors as The Rosaries. Prayer Beads seemed an accurate characterization, for their jagged coast lay littered with the broken shells of many vessels captained by unwary mariners who had strayed into the treacherous cross-currents and been dashed against the shores.

To pass these islands, and to help combat the sideways drift such as had occurred during my trial runs, I had fitted a temporary keel between the two hulls, formed by a large sheet of sea-ply. All along the Colombian coast meandering currents run in every direction, and I needed this extra depth to give me added maneuverability. Such deep keels are never permanent fixtures on catamarans. The characteristic figure-8 roll of twin hulls causes stresses that either tear the hulls apart or rip the keel off. Mono-hulled yachts are a different matter. They pivot naturally on their single keel, and although there is still a lot of pressure, it is applied against one surface at a time.

As the Caribbean swell became more pronounced, I could hear the splintering of wood as the plywood construction flexed and warped like a *punkah* fan. The keel swung between the hulls, just a few inches at first, then a full foot as the wood became weaker.

We must have passed through a plankton-rich sea-feeding-ground, for phosphorescent spores swirled around the square-tipped keel-ends in turbulent twisting whorls. Lengthening cracks in the wood gleamed as phosphorous debris became embedded in long lines of cracks, there to be starkly offset by the invisible sections that remained as black as the unlit sea.

Soon the cracks had spread, multi-fingered, from either plywood side, often overlapping as though broken completely through. The keel still prevented a fair amount of drift, but after some four hours and ten miles, most of its strength was gone. However, I was satisfied that it had achieved its main purpose. I was far from the bay and shore and well past the danger-zone of the Rosarios.

As though to authenticate my thoughts a ship's light showed brightly from eastward. It crossed my stern and disappeared, paralleling the coast in a westerly direction. Two white masthead-lights and a green starboard light, with a few faint deck-lights amidships, were all I could distinguish. It was probably a local fishing vessel without radar or proper lookouts. It gave no indication of seeing me, for neither of my lights was lit.

When on watch, I use lights as seldom as possible, for they destroy night-vision, making it difficult to steer by the stars or to detect advancing breaking waves. If I do see a ship that seems headed on a collision course, I steer to clear its path.

It was a beautiful night, neither hot nor cold, and the sky was as bright as though lit by candles. Even though I knew I should get a good night's sleep, I did not feel tired. The soothing breeze of the trade winds was intoxicating, and my excitement was added to by the fact that this was my first night at sea. Nevertheless, I knew the importance of that extra reservoir of alertness, so often necessary at a moment's notice, and decided, reluctantly, to go below.

I lit a kerosene hurricane-light and left it burning brightly in the starboard mizzen rigging. From aft the light would be clearly visible. From forward the light would shine through the sails, giving equal notice. I left the cabin hatch open as I made myself comfortable on my foam-rubber mattress. The unruffled progress of the stars as they moved across the blue-black sky told me my course was true.

Surprisingly, I fell asleep almost at once. I must have been more tired than I had thought, and it was broad daylight when I awoke. It had been a short night's sleep, but a thorough one. I had slept as soundly as I had ever slept. The rocking motion and murmuring slap of the sea against the hull had been almost hypnotic, and the accumulated aches and tenseness of the past month's work had completely disappeared. The Sierra Sagrada almost looked as smug as I when I came atop its decks just as the sun rose over the horizon.

The only trouble was that I awoke with a crink in the back of my neck and found that a pair of pliers had slipped beneath the mattress. This was a hazard of a single-surface deck: everything not weighty enough to find its own grip tends to slip or slide from one end of the craft to the other. Fortunately, they slipped backward as well as forward, and when they had made the rounds, I picked them up and replaced them on their own hook or in their cubicle.

I stretched as I waited for a navigation time-check. I noted the time, 0658 hours, as the sun's tip peeked over the horizon. This was my first entry in the red notebook that substituted for a ship's log. This routine taken care of, I paid attention to the remains of last night's false-keel, which now lay almost completely shattered under the *Sierra Sagrada*'s hull.

The roll of the *Sierra Sagrada* was much smoother now that the keel was broken. I tried to work the quick-release bolts loose, but they had jammed with the stress that had been placed against them, and I was forced to use my ax to chop the broken sea-ply clear, inch by inch and piece by piece. Red-painted chips and slithers trailed behind in my wake. Then, with a final rip, the main sheet twisted free of its own volition, swirled away into the stream and was left behind.

"If a passing fishing vessel picks it up, they'll say the *Sierra Sagrada* foundered," I thought aloud, for bets had been made among the visitors of the club that I would not survive 24 hours.

The wind had changed course during the night, and I had been about 15 degrees off course when I awoke. I therefore tightened the sails and eased the tiller to bring me to a more easterly bearing as soon as I came on deck. Now, when the broken keel fell free, the change of balance made me veer further east. After waiting for the *Sierra Sagrada* to settle on its true course, I once more reset the sails—which, I found, were close to their original position.

I had drawn a line on my chart directly between Cartagena and the Yucatan Straits, with the avowed intention of keeping strictly to windward. This gave me clear deep water to starboard for many days and left the potentially dangerous reefs and shallows to port. Cayman Island would have been an ideal in-between destination to have aimed for, but my skimpy sails were too small and low to close-haul into the northeast trades. Indeed, even properly rigged yachts often have to tack, or make use of their auxiliary motors, to reach Cayman Island's shelter.

During the night I had noticed how the grinding sound of the loose-link chain around the hull had faded to an occasional clink as the straps had settled to their final positions, and I was not to hear any more sound from them. The tightening nuts also were firm, and the only adjustments I had to make were to the rigging, which had worked itself loose under the initial stretching of the sail.

The morning was bright and sunny, and a feeling of elation overwhelmed me as I searched the horizon and saw I had left land far behind. No other craft was in sight; I had the whole sea to myself. A few stray gulls wheeled high overhead, and a frigate bird mooched along above my masts. I almost felt I was a part of their world.

Breakfast was boiled eggs and leftovers of the chicken from last night's supper. Automatically, I shaved. I expected no visitors, but I was easing myself into the journey slowly.

The sound of the wind and the waves was magnified by my being alone. Music still came in loud and clear, and I turned the radio up. My wristwatch was left hanging on a hook inside the cabin, and I uncoiled into a comfortable place near the tiller and relaxed.

A few small fish found shelter under my hulls' shade, and I leaned over to make acquaintance with my new visitors. They were only small fish, hardly larger than sticklebacks, and their tails and fins beat with windmill speed to keep abreast. Shelter is a hard thing to find in the deep sea, and these little fish had no intention of letting me get away, for there even the ever-hungry frigate birds could not reach them, although they kept a beady eye overhead.

Like a Chinese store, my decks were laden with tackle and provisions. Cans of water sat before the cabin, and lashed alongside were woven baskets with potatoes, cabbage, oranges and other vegetables and fruit. A stem of bananas hung from my mizzen rigging, and a sack of green coconuts was stored amidships for later in the voyage. The brisk sea air gave me a healthy appetite.

Cooking was supposed to be a daily affair, with a blue-flame cooker sitting in a gimballed box on the cabin-top. However, good ideas go astray, and the stove was left to rust unused when I found I had no need for hot food.

Instead of feeling lonesome, I now felt king of my own domain. I had no other boats around me to make my craft seem small. And although my decks were less than a dozen steps from bow to stern, I had no feeling of being hemmed in. For a roof I had the whole sky, and nothing can be bigger than that. For the walls I had the sea, which would also serve as a larder if need be. With my hat pushed over my eyes, I leaned against my swinging tiller and dozed as the sun climbed its lazy way upward.

My craft was patterned after Polynesian outriggers, which rode the vast Pacific Ocean's trade routes on regular schedules for a thousand years and more. In ancient days

the Polynesians used straps of bark and vine to hold their
catamarans together, and many of their smaller craft are
still that way today. Breaking seas swirl through the open
framework of their craft, reducing stress to a minimum.
The *Sierra Sagrada* was built on the self-same principles.

I had learned a lesson the hard way about the respective
merits of modern materials and old ideas.

When I had hiked across Panama's Darien from west to
east, I had been stranded at the end of the trail at the top of
the Chuquanaqui River. There I had bought a canoe to
take me downstream. No large canoes were available, and I
had been forced to buy an unbalanced medicine-canoe.

To provide balance, Ari Mastali, the Cuna *brujo,* the
local wizard, had lashed on an outrigger using split-vines.
When he had gone, I had condescendingly changed these
for 300-pound breaking-strain nylon cord. But Ari Mastali
had been right. A day on the river and my nylon had
stretched and retightened a dozen times. That first night
I had cut down creepers from tall trees in the surrounding
jungle, split the creepers in two and soaked the coils in the
river overnight. The next day I relashed my canoe. I had no
further trouble. By coincidence, my first Cuna canoe was
bought less than 100 miles from where my present San Blas
canoe was made.

As the day went by, I became more relaxed. A cargo
ship appeared over the horizon behind me and proceeded
to pass within a 100 yards of the *Sierra Sagrada* without
apparently noticing me. In mild retaliation I went below
and went through yesterday's newspapers.

Time was no problem. I had no boss, no clock-card to
punch, no calendar to watch. My course was set, and now I
just had to sail it. Once past the vagrant tides and eddies I

had no further worries. From my present position a strong beam wind combined with a 0.9 knot current would take me almost automatically through the Straits of Yucatan. The Serrano Bank and the Roncador Bank were in my vicinity, but I should pass 50 miles well to their east.

Navigation presented an interesting challenge. I had once crossed the Atlantic using only sunrise and sunset and a nautical almanac and time (synchronized by my transistor radio). My system had proved accurate and was to prove accurate again. But friends who knew nothing about sailing said, "What would you have done without a nautical almanac."

I thought this an excellent opportunity to find out.

May 5 sunrise at Cartagena was 0544 hours. Sunset 1814 hours. This meant the length of the day from sunrise to sunset was 12 hours 30 minutes long. May 10, five days later, sunrise was 0543 hours and sunset 1831 hours, or 12 hours 48 minutes apart. Naturally, the length of the day grew longer as I traveled further north.

I made a note:

|        | Sunrise | Sunset | Length of Day     |
|--------|---------|--------|-------------------|
| May  5 | 0544    | 1814   | 12 hrs. 30 min.   |
| May 10 | 0543    | 1831   | 12 hrs. 48 min.   |

This showed me that sunrise on May 10 was one minute earlier than when I set out. Sunset was seventeen minutes later. A quick calculation showed me that, in nautical terms, I had traveled approximately 120 miles westward.

If I had stayed on the same Cartagena longitude of 75° 30′ west, sunrise on May 10 would have been nine minutes earlier and sunset nine minutes later than on May 5. But I did not have a nautical almanac with me to tell me exact sunrise/sunset times, so latitude was still a guess. However,

I estimated I was traveling roughly 50 miles a day, and my estimation later proved accurate. I had a pilot chart of the Caribbean, and this was sufficient for me to know where land was.

My compass was of the simplest kind, for cash was too short to spend it frivolously and I bought six 8-cent compasses on the assumption—valid, I was sure!—that 8 cents or $80, all compasses point north. (Four of these compasses rusted through. One I inadvertently sat on. The other, still in mint condition, is a souvenir in Chicago.)

The Caribbean became a deep-green, with long rolling waves built high and smooth by the prevailing trade winds. Sargasso weed streamed in floating banners on the surface, and small fish sought refuge in increasing numbers under my hull. The daytime radio stations faded, and I was forced to take a new look at my surroundings.

At one time a school of green dolphins came swimming alongside the *Sierra Sagrada*'s hulls. They had never seen such a craft before, and they darted and splashed beneath the canoes while I lay sprawled on the deck. Soon one dolphin realized the twin hulls formed a tunnel of calm water, and he made a half-circle at the stern and thrashed through at full bore. Another started to follow his example but nervously dived deeper as he approached. And so it would go. The variety of sea life is unending. One can never be bored.

May 12 I was in my cabin when I heard the heavy throb of an approaching ship. I looked out to see the Danish freighter *Magleby Maersk* making a circle around me, checking to see if I needed assistance. I waved a greeting to say I was all right, and they waved back from their tall white bridge and went westward on their way.

The *Sierra Sagrada* took me along perfectly. My sails were schooner rig, with side-by-side jibs leading to each of the bows. I had intended to make one jib only, but when I cut the canvas from corner to corner, I found I had two identical jibs. The idea was too good to overlook, and the ensuing side-by-side jibs behaved perfectly. By adjusting the mizzen and jibs I could sail automatically over practically any course I chose. My only problem was the wind, for the sails were too small.

The *Sierra Sagrada* was not the fastest of craft, but people who want to sail fast should not buy dugout canoes for hulls. Nor was it the most comfortable craft. But it could go up the shallowest rivers, run safely on a beach, bounce tranquilly over reef or shallows or sit out a howling gale. Unless the *Sagrada* was terribly overloaded, I always had the same complaint. "Everything went right" is fine as far as travel is concerned, but it's disastrous for writing.

I was traveling steadily northwest, expecting to pass through the Straits of Yucatan, when the trade winds started veering. First, the wind dropped. Then squalls came up out of the north and west. I tacked to make as much headway as possible, but I was running into a series of back-to-back rainstorms. Soon these erratic winds became worse. A gust from the north, then a squall from the west, followed by light airs from the south. All afternoon and into the night I tried to gain a mile or two, checking the floating Sargasso weed to estimate which way the currents flowed in an effort to gain the modicum of distance that would ease my mind. At least, I could think that I was making gains in a favorable direction.

I could not set my sails on automatic that night, for the chances were equally divided that I would go in either direction. Every two hours, it seemed, the wind gyrated in swirling eddies, boxing the compass from north to south and back to north again.

The winds faded during the night, and I awakened next morning to the uncanny sound of utter silence. Not a timber or spar squeaked. The sea was flat, and the sails hung limp as a Sunday wash. When I untied the tiller, it was so unmoving that I could have balanced an egg on the tiller-post.

Clearly the weather was breaking. A storm was brewing.

For four days this calm persisted. On the second day two 1,000-foot-high waterspouts danced across the sea, but by the time I had noticed their presence and raced on deck to batten-down the sails, they had dissipated their energy in tiny whirlwinds, which briefly flecked the sea to whitened suds before allowing it to calm to glassy smoothness once more.

I had been steering the *Sierra Sagrada* to pass the western tip of Cuba, as far from the dangerous shoals of Yucatan as possible yet a fair distance from the potential hazards of Fidel Castro's island. I had no wish to be involved in politics, and the only reports I had heard from Cuba had not been encouraging.

I was carrying two flags aboard the *Sierra Sagrada*, the Stars and Stripes and the red, yellow and green of Colombia. Surreptitiously I took the Stars and Stripes down and placed my British passport in a convenient position: diplomacy can save a lot of headaches.

But I had no cause to worry. Contrary winds took me east of the Isle of Pines to a group of barren islands inhabited only by hundreds of three-foot-long iguanas and millions of black-striped mosquitoes. I was certainly more welcome to the mosquitoes than they were to me; they zoomed in as though they had not had a decent meal in months, and I swatted them by the bushel.

White coral sand, encrusted with scarlet starfish, lay three feet below the emerald-green sea. Three-inch mussel-shells shone like pearls in the glittering waters, and yellow-banded tiger-fish harmonized against sea urchins and other multicolored life. Slowly I traversed this whole coral-garden, which covered a score of square miles.

With no prospect of moving further while the inclement weather lasted, I went exploring along the beach, and snorkeling in the refreshing waters. It was a pretty island, but although I seldom am lonely, I began to yearn for company. Up in the mountains looking at a well-favored panorama, or eating an outstandingly well-prepared meal, or sipping a fine wine—sometimes one needs to share the good things in life. This cay was one of these places. I would never have found it if a calm had not cast me there, and I wanted to share it.

Company of a sort did arrive. Three Cubans stayed briefly at the island. "Fishermen," they called themselves. "Look! We have lobsters!" they said. Nevertheless, they arrived in the dark from the direction of Grand Cayman Island and were distinctly surprised to awaken next morning and find they had anchored near me. They emphatically wanted no photographs taken, and I respected their desire for confidence, wishing them happy smuggling as they went on their way.

A sign of the troubled times was the presence of unlit planes, which flew back and forth in the direction of Guatemala. I saw or heard them on several nights and tried to guess their country of origin. I never did reach a conclusion.

The stormy weather in my vicinity was becoming more intense. While the squalls blew from the northwest, I was protected by the cay. But sitting out the weather was not enough. I wanted to make headway, a feeling reinforced when the weather-front reversed itself, and gusty squalls came blasting in off the open sea, leaving me completely vulnerable to any heavier winds.

Finally, rather than risk staying any longer, and reluctant to look for a more sheltered site, I bounced out to sea on twin jibs and mizzen, literally heading from squall to squall until out of sight of land. Eventually, however, the squalls merged into one rollicking tempest, and on the following day Miami weather bureau let shipping know that Hurricane Alma was on its way. If I had had a transmitter aboard, I could have scooped the story, for I had been soaked by its long-fingered froth for 24 hours.

June is supposed to be a fine month for weather, and Alma was something of a freak for triggering the hurricane season to such an early start. The official season does not start until July. But clearly Alma was not deterred by being premature as it followed hurricane alley across Cuba and Florida to the North Atlantic Ocean. Over Dry Tortuga Island it was clocked at 125 knots, and it caused damage amounting to many millions of dollars.

The *Sierra Sagrada* sat so low in the water that the very height of the waves protected me. Only when I reached the peak of a wave would I be lashed by the wind, and then I would have respite as we roller-coasted the length of the swell down to another protected valley.

Yet the difficulties were not without their severity. For example, I found that when I was sailing under bare masts alone, the tiller was continually wrenched from my hands as the stern lurched sideways in a sudden downward skid over a short-cresting wave. In fact, the rudder thrashed around so violently I was scared it would tear itself apart. Moreover, since breaking seas were falling in from astern, I reasoned it would be wise to try to move a little faster. Consequently, after 30 minutes' sail with bare rigging, I labored forward to hoist one of the jibs, with a heaving-line tied around my waist for safety. Once the jib was up again, the wind, a 65-knot "eddy," took grip, and the *Sierra Sagrada* responded with a surge. The bow wave literally hissed as I clambered back to the cockpit's safety, and we whistled through the Straits of Yucatan in fine style, anxious only lest the jib rip to shreds. Until it did so, however, I reasoned that there was nothing I could do, so, with power to spare, I lashed the tiller and set the *Sierra Sagrada* on an automatic course. The halyards billowed out as if pregnant, and the straining jib stretched so tight that it shone. Then, since the stinging rain was icy cold and so thick at times that I could scarcely see the bow, I closed the hatch doors and huddled in the cabin, letting the hurricane do its damnedest. There was not much it could do. A heavier craft would have been torn to pieces, but I rode each capricious wave like a cork.

Night time was the worst, a bedlam of howling winds and crashing waves. The *Sierra Sagrada* shuddered every time a flying sea hit, then whimpered for a full 30 seconds, until the next wave came along.

I had been soaked long since, and now sat hunched in a parka and a blanket listening to Radio Miami.

" . . . a storm warning for southern Florida, western Cuba and adjacent waters," a blasé voice recited. "Residents are advised to stay at home and stay tuned-in to this station for future developments."

It hardly seemed likely that any new news would be good news, so I turned the radio off, checked to see the jib was still in one piece and went to sleep for a couple of hours.

The dawn broke gray and drizzly, but the wind was down to 30 knots. The previously sturdy jib was now in shreds, but the *Sierra Sagrada* had made more headway in the previous 24 hours than it was ever to make again.

Hindsight makes me look favorably at Hurricane Alma, for it sped me into the Gulf of Mexico before the weather-pattern broke once more, and I was left becalmed 300 miles closer to my destination.

The winds had hardly abated before storm-tossed birds and insects took refuge on my decks. Dragonflies clung to the rope-lashings. Mosquitoes I sprayed with Flit. A bank-swallow stayed all night and well into the next day eating brine-soaked biscuits on the cabin roof, while a tern passed the same night perched on the upper point of my outrigger's stern.

The following calm lasted more than a week. Hurricanes are like that: first a calm, then a hurricane, then a calm. Currents pass through the Gulf of Mexico before branching east and west at the Louisiana coast, and while the calm persisted this current was my only means of propulsion.

A blue sky and a burning sun tempted me to be in the water more often than I was on deck. Swimming while sailing is suicidal, but we were becalmed, and the few light winds that occasionally rippled the sails were scarcely worth bothering about. I would be losing very few miles' travel if I wasted them. So I lowered the sail, stripped to swimming shoes and snorkel and went over the side. The water was smooth and transparently clear. The surface was a pleasant 85 degrees, while 10 feet and deeper it dropped to a nippy 65 degrees.

Cartagena waterfront.

Voters being searched before being allowed to cast their ballots in the elections.

Fitting decking and cabin to the Santa Marta canoe.

Dry rot in the San Blas canoe.

Preparing to raise the masts on the *Sierra Sagrada*.

*Sierra Sagrada* fully rigged.

Crossing the Caribbean.

Sailing on "automatic"—with tiller tied.

Pump led to outrigger. My main hull could be emptied in any weather—though usually a wipe with a sponge was sufficient.

Starfish in Caribbean shallows.

*Above.* The *Magleby Maersk* in the Caribbean.

*Right.* Perfect sunrises and sunsets occurred every four days.

*Below.* Knives, forks, camera, watch, spare compasses — everything had its own place.

*Above.* Shark in the Caribbean.

*Left.* Sargosso weed.

*Bottom left.* The cheapest compasses proved adequate.

*Below.* One of the fish snagged with a 6-prong hook.

The *Sierra Sagrada* beneath the *Sprague* at Vicksburg.

Arrival at Chicago.

Light marine growth had appeared on the hull bottoms. It didn't slow progress yet, but mosses and barnacles can grow at fantastic rates once they have secured a hold. I hoed the underwater hulls smooth with a metal blade and knife, then scrubbed the remainder clean. One hundred feet below I could still see the tiny shells glistening as they streamed to the bottom.

Robust flying fish and tuna blurred my vision in their eagerness to snatch the tiny flotsam, and even pointed jabs in their tough hides would make them pause only long enough to give me a pained look of surprise as they darted aside.

Sharks and green dolphins were a different matter. As soon as they came within view, I swung topside until the sea was clear again. Only once did I go overboard without taking a lengthy look around first, and then I came eyeball to eyeball with a five-foot shark. The meeting was brief: the shark panicked into the depths; I panicked back on deck again.

The craziest fish to follow me was a basking sawfish, which waved its six-foot-long proboscis with such abandon that I was thankful nature has not yet evolved an electric variety. "I saw him, but he didn't saw me," I noted in my log.

Heat or cold was not a problem on the *Sierra Sagrada*. The water temperature around the hull remained constant, warming the craft at night and cooling it in the day. On favorable days, when a light wind blew, the spray kept me refreshed, as though the boat were air-conditioned, in even the hottest scorches.

Fishing has never been an exceptionally strong point with me. Canned sardines are my usual limit. Earlier in the voyage I had tried to catch tuna with hook and line, but they had broken my line and straightened my hooks, and I never had heaved one on deck. Now, on constant alert and with nothing better to do, I tried an older method. I fashioned a six-pronged hook and used it to jab at the smaller fishes about the boat, sticking at their tails, noses or fins, or at whatever went by. By the end of the day I had a fair-sized mess of fish.

My kerosene stove had been of the thinnest tin and had long since been discarded, thus I had no way to cook. But I did have something else. When I was leaving Cartagena, Dan Lundberg had gone to the *Passat,* brought forth a bottle of brandy and passed it over to me to drink a toast to the voyage. This is scarcely a sensible thing to do when a ship is about to leave port, and I had carelessly placed it on my deck and forgotten to give it back. I later saw Dan waving frantically on the dock, and I thought he was waving good-bye. Only later did I realize he was yelling for me to bring back his brandy.

Ill-gotten gains are a dastardly thing. In this case the cork had become loosened, and the brandy was ruined with salt water. But rather than throw it away, I had kept it as a genuine medicinal reserve, and now I decided to marinate the raw fish I had caught. I steeped a couple of them in the brandy overnight, but the result was not a success. As a change of diet the fish tasted no worse than any other raw fish and barely better than salt-spoiled brandy. It is not a receipe I would recommend.

Gradually, as I made my way northward, the stringy Sargasso weed changed direction and shape. Where it had flowed in long straight lines up to now, a pattern characteristic of a smoothly flowing current, now it was breaking into isolated clumps, which suggested I had run into a series of eddies and that, therefore, I might be sighting land soon.

Then a reef-eel emerged one day, and shore birds became commonplace. The voice of Herb Holiday of New Orleans's WWL came over the airwaves, and I prepared to look for land.

The whole sea around me was changing. All the green dolphins had disappeared, as had most of the other deep-sea fish. The water beneath me changed from blue to dark green and then to light green as I neared the shallowing coastal waters. Soon I was under the influence of the land winds, and I could feel the actual grit in the air as the wind veered from the west.

I shaved my beard and used a spare five-gallon drum of water to wash the salt from my clothes. For the first time in weeks I became concerned about the *Sierra Sagrada*'s appearance, and I hoisted the Stars and Stripes in case the authorities in charge wondered who would be nearing their shores with a pair of dugout canoes.

Toward late afternoon I saw a homeward-bound fishing trawler, and I asked him my position. I had been 44 days at sea, and I was in no mood to start guessing. Great was my astonishment, therefore, when he yelled back, "The Mississippi is dead ahead!"

Radio, compass and pilot chart had brought me to where I had aimed!

There were still a few miles to go. I sailed ahead, and by midnight the flickering glare of burning gases from offshore oil rigs had appeared. There were so many rigs and so many lights that I could not tell sea from shore, so against this background, I dropped anchor and stayed overnight.

The sun had not even risen when I weighed anchor and started on my way. Four hundred yards to my west lay the Southwest-Pass Lighthouse. I sailed over to try to make a landing, but the swift-flowing Mississippi current threatened to carry me out to sea. I could make no headway against the five-knot current, and the passing trawler *Prowler* towed me across to the nearby Coast Guard station at the lighthouse base.

After customs and immigration officials had given me clearance, I caught a ride with them to New Orleans, where I bought a used 20-horsepower Mercury motor for $200. It was not a wise investment, for the motor blew a rod after battling the current for less than 30 minutes, and once more I was in danger of being swirled out to sea.

The Coast Guard auxiliary *Gray Ghost* captained by Dick McConnell saw my predicament and towed me as far as Venice, Louisiana, where there was an excellent motor-repair workshop. Sail-powered dugouts are useless things to sail up the Mississippi, and I sat wondering whether to repair my motor or to buy a new one. Bud Latham, who ran a boat service to the outlying oil rigs, settled the matter, when he offered me a new 20-horsepower Johnson motor.

"Sure will do the job nicely," I said. "But I will not need it after I reach Chicago."

"Fine. Send it back," said Bud.

Johnson Motors went one better. They sent Bud Latham a new replacement and used the original to prove the toughness of their product.

Venice had been hit by Hurricane Betsy the year before; the surging Mississippi had rolled over the levees and combined with the tempestuous winds to destroy most of the homes. Venice was still a trailer town, and inland there were still boats aground that had been swirled ashore by the inundating waters. But if the town was far from rebuilt, it was well on the way to recovery.

Shrimp were the main thing I remembered in Venice harbor. A fishing boat with a group of cursing fishermen came limping in with a rope snarled around its propeller, and the owner and I prepared to dive underneath to cut it free.

There were only five feet of water, so depth was no problem. But the shrimp were so hungry and numerous and nipped so sharply that I came topside and donned beach shoes, long trousers, shirt and snorkel before going down with a knife again.

Shrimp boats use outspread mesh butterfly nets and catch shrimp by the ton. In exchange for my help, I was given my fill of the small creatures. They made for a pleasant evening, for shrimp is one of the few sea-foods I like.

The Caribbean was behind me, and I stowed my sails and whipped the running-rigging to my fore and mizzen masts. I would not be using them again. It would be motor from now onward.

# Chapter IV

THE JOURNEY across the Caribbean had taken me 45 days, and the journey upriver would take me a month more. Huckleberry Finn would never recognize the river now. Winding waters and towheads with cottonwood trees still dominate the scene, but the United States Corps of Engineers have straightened many kinks in the river and dredged the bars between the pools, so that today the current fairly gallops instead of "strolling along."

Now I was seeing landbirds instead of seabirds, geese instead of pelicans, hawks instead of gulls. Five groups of birds, in perfect diagonal formation, glided in from the shore. It was a calm and serene day. Then the leader flapped its wings, disturbing the airflow. So the second followed suit, then the third, then the fourth, until the fifth had to flap frantically to remain in formation.

Much the same happened with me. I would hug the bank of the Mississippi as close as possible, where the slower currents lay, but then an ocean-size freighter would churn upstream, sending me bouncing around in its wake, until the river's edge became serene again.

Not until I reached New Orleans did I feel as though the Caribbean part of my cruise had been left behind. And as I chugged through its busy suburbs and wound my way past 10,000-ton ships sunk by Hurricane Betsy, I realized that, in many ways, it was more dangerous to be on the river than to be at sea. Beyond New Orleans I tied up for the night against an embankment of transport barges—and promptly had the forward end of my Cuna canoe knocked off by a shifting barge.

Higher up river the current slowed, and by Baton Rouge it was only two or three knots, enabling me to browse through bayous and flooded creeks. It was a shame I could not have stayed around longer, for every few miles a new creek presented itself.

Rather than tie up in marinas, I anchored along the river bank. The barnacle fuzz that I had acquired in the Caribbean leeched off under the fresh water action, and soon my hulls were as clean as when I had started out.

I was not the only unconventional craft on the river. At Memphis, looking for gasoline, I motored into the Memphis Yacht Club and tied up alongside a three-pontooned contraption that almost made my craft look conventional. It belonged to Eldon Brandley. Eldon and son Tylor and Douglas King were on their way to New Orleans from Indiana. Eldon, at least, was making a far more practical journey: he was going downstream.

Memphis was the first big town I had stayed at since I had left Cartagena, and the four of us took in a movie on Beale Street.

"Anything, as long as it is not a sea story," was my only request, and Eldon shared the same sentiments. We chose a Western.

Greenboro and Memphis. New London and Cairo.

These were names I had only heard before. At New London I took time out to write letters to Chicago, to tell my friends I was coming.

The currrent south of Cairo, at the junction of the Mississippi and the Ohio Rivers, is a mass of swirling pools. Coasting downstream with the current was a 14-foot runabout with two fishermen frantically working on their motor.

"Want a hand?" I yelled over.

"We'd prefer a tow," they shouted back.

I took my towing rope from my bow and tied it to the stern, and they made fast behind me. John Wills and his friend had been on the river two hours since their motor had broken down, and they had already come to rue the fact they did not have any oars with which to paddle to the banks. I towed them to the mouth of a nearby creek, and between us we diagnosed a flooded carburetor and dry spark plugs. And in no time, I had their motor going.

They offered to pay me for my work, but I told them I had not paid my own debts off yet. I offered them a tow upstream, but then they saw fishes bite on their still trailing fishing line. John drawled he wouldn't be going anywhere for a while. I left them hauling up catfish and continued on my way.

The river current once more increased as we headed through the narrowing river to St. Louis. Wing-dams had been placed along both sides of the banks to keep the channel racing through the center, and at one stage the current speed matched my cruising speed and I was brought to a complete halt, but then I detected a chain of swirling turbulence where two channel currents formed. Jockeying into position, I eased upstream on the slight back-currents until I reached more favorable water.

When I reached St. Louis, all the hard work was over. I checked my log from New Orleans to St. Louis center, and found it had taken me 22 days of steady plodding from sunrise to sunset. Old records showed that the *Robert E. Lee* took only 3 days, 18 hours and 14 minutes when it raced the *Natchez* in July, 1870. Perhaps progress over the past century has not been as great as I had thought.

An odd thing happened at St. Louis when I was looking for gasoline and oil. The river map I was using was a couple of years old, and it showed the St. Louis Yacht Club, whose address I had used in the past, as a favorable refill station. But as I cruised up and down the river between Municipal Bridge and McKinley Bridge looking for this elusive club, I drew a blank. In desperation I motored over to a gasoline competitor to ask for directions.

"It sank," I was told.

"Impossible," I declared. "Yacht clubs don't sink."

But I was wrong. The St. Louis Yacht Club had been situated on a converted barge, and the barge had sunk at its moorings. And each time the barge had been on the verge of being salvaged, the river had risen and the St. Louis Yacht Club had sunk again.

Perhaps St. Louis has a submarine club now.

I must admit that my favorite part of the river was past Alton, for after Alton the Mississippi follows the picturesque pools of the dammed river. Then, too, the dams slow the current to less than one knot—which made me feel that I was no longer running uphill all the way. I also realized the end was soon.

From the Mississippi I branched off into the Illinois

River and anchored at picnic grounds instead of by swirling streams.

"What are these things?" kids would say, as they climbed aboard.

"Hollow logs," I'd answer. "And they came from South America."

"You kidding?" they would say. Only the blowguns and grass-skirts in the hold authenticated my tall stories.

Even then many thought I was soft-selling a movie or television show. But they would take photographs. And I would take photographs of them. And someone would take photographs of me taking photographs of them. And so it went on. The *Sierra Sagrada* was a popular boat.

The fact my hulls were hollow logs was stunningly impressed when mushrooms started growing the outside length of my Santa Marta hull. Fresh water combined with the summer sun had revitalized the spores that had lain dormant since its days in the South American jungle. I scrubbed the hull with Lysol to bring the growth under control, but all I did was send them to sleep again, for I was to meet them later in the journey.

When I arrived at last in Chicago, the Field Museum gave me a royal welcome, even though they had bought the craft sight unseen, and I suspected they did not entirely approve of my style of delivery. After all, most artifacts are sent by freight.

As I tied up at Burnham Harbor in Chicago and passed my proud craft to a new command, all Don Collier could say was, "We expected him to send it, not bring it."

# Chapter V

THE CANOES were left on museum display at Stanley Field Hall, and kids especially seemed to like the exhibit. But it seemed somewhat out of place, for Chicago's Field Museum specializes in things of a more serious nature, localized artifacts, plants, outlines of cultures and research, and things other than sea-going yachts. The *Sierra Sagrada* in its present state did not fall into any of their categories.

My original intention had been to take the craft apart when I reached Chicago, but I must admit that during the journey I had grown attached to its ugly-duckling appearance and I was pleased to see it was still in one piece. Weekly I went to the museum to browse around, and I sometimes sat awed kids on its red-hued land-dry cabin and let them pretend they were at sea.

Some of the other artifacts I had collected I also left on exhibit. The grass skirts of the Yaguas and the beaten-bark blankets were especially well received, for it seemed I had been fortunate to secure especially fine examples.

Other artifacts I kept to festoon my apartment. Or to show at lectures. Or to pass on to friends who were professionally active at some of the Chicago-area universities.

One group of blowguns I had with me when I visited the O'Keefes, a group of friends so close I became almost one of the family. And it was then that the O'Keefes and Jack Reynolds and I decided on a blowgun-shoot at the Reynolds farm to subdue a group of obnoxious pigeons that had taken residence in their barn. We passed out blowguns and darts and shot until the beams sprouted like porcupines. But either the pigeons were too wily or our marksmanship was not the best, for the pigeons remained completely safe.

"Don't sit over there, Frank," Tom shouted, and I saw a curare-tipped dart sticking out of another bale of hay.

We packed up our blowguns, and left the pigeons once more in peace.

It was also time to go back to work again, to replenish my flattened bank balance. My journeys are always paid for by myself, and if they do not reach their hoped-for financial return, then I have to work to balance the difference.

My place for employment for the past few years had been La Salle Photofinishing. This was the busy time of the year, and Bill Yamamoto was happy to have me back. Work is something I like doing; my only complaint is that it takes up so much valuable time. Summer work is six days a week, for photographs have to be printed in a hurry, and Bill maintained an unusually high quality control—which meant no short cuts and twice as much work to get out as the normal season.

My job was on a color printing machine, an electronic printer/enlarger that makes postcard-sized prints from any size negatives. Like everything else, it is a simple machine to use once you know how to use it, and I had once owned a similar (but much more primitive) enlarger in my own business.

I am always fascinated to see what other people are doing with their lives and leisure time, and my photographic work is sometimes like a running travelogue: photo-finishing can be a very compatible profession.

Concurrently with operating the enlarger I would mull over past and future plans. Small details that had escaped my notice swam into focus as they were juxtaposed with seemingly irrelevant features as the jungle and sea journeys merged into one. And as the pattern consolidated and stabilized, I saw clearly that what at first seemed opposed and incongruous was in reality consonant.

I found life in Chicago confusing, in a pleasant sort of way. Work and vacation are only relative, and I was presently at a loss to know which was which. Whatever the case, it kept me on a very tight schedule.

Sometimes I gave lectures of my South American journeys, for my slides had proved more interesting than I had expected. Further technical aspects of the artifacts and fungus samples I had collected for the Hektoen Institute of Cook County Hospital had also to be checked. In fact, I was kept very busy as one month rolled into another.

We had parties; we had squabbles. Misunderstandings came and went. Sometimes emotions ran high in the morning and were torpedoed in the afternoon. Other times work seemed a waste of time, a feeling offset only when paycheck-day came around. Then work did not seem so bad after all. Even boredom crept in and hung around, until I kicked myself out of the stupor. In other words, it was a normal healthy routine.

And like other normal, healthy routine employees, I set my goal ahead for next year's summer.

Projects are the least of my problems. I have a long list of things I would like to do, for every journey seems to en-

courage two new ideas. To make my journeys as economical
as possible, I make outlines of my aims, then shuffle them
together so one journey-section supports the other. In this
way journeys overlap, and while one stage is being completed, another is being prepared.

Small craft sailing seemed a good idea, but I had no
specific sea voyages in mind. And more often my mind
turned to another plan, one that involved flying a balloon
across land masses. In this way, I thought I could browse
and photograph in comfort, without the bother of controls
and places to camp or land.

My complacency about ballooning, however, was rudely
shattered when I brought the whole project under closer
scrutiny and found it complicated by whole books of adverse
rules and regulations. Even more important, a balloon is
a contrary thing, beset about by thermals and down-
draughts and other forces not encountered in everyday
sailing.

Still the idea persisted. And I merely substituted the
idea of a tethered balloon traveling over sea in place of a free
balloon flying over land.

I made a model from paper and suspended it in my
apartment. Facts and figures I devoured. But as I made a
check on all the major balloon flights, I found that honest,
down-to-earth information was hard to obtain. I looked in
the books in the libraries and stores but found no written
record of the type of craft I had in mind: a balloon 50 feet
by 50 feet, tethered to the sea by means of a trailing float, its
basket suspended some 100 feet above the ocean. It would
be a kind of kite in the air, or perhaps a detached sail would
be a more accurate description.

As I have said before, no journey is valid as far as I am
concerned unless every reasonable precaution is taken. And

I therefore formulated two general stipulations: (1) the balloon must not be a navigational hazard; (2) safety factors had to be so stringent that no unnecessary danger to life or limb would be involved.

Lake Michigan would be large enough to test the theory, but the Atlantic Ocean seemed even better. A balloon journey across Lake Michigan would be great for a weekend, but if the journey was to pay for itself, I needed a project that would tie-in with other ideas. Tiptoeing around is not one of my major accomplishments, so I marshaled facts and figures and waded in.

The nucleus of the new journey took shape. As navigator and steersman I would ride in a basket high above the waves, secured in a conventional manner to the neck of the balloon, which would have a surface area of 2,500 square feet, trailing a 200-pound float behind.

Take-off site would have to be determined later, but it would be somewhere off the African coast. Destination would be the Caribbean, and I would try controlling the balloon with the aid of a bridle attached to the balloon sac and the trailing rope.

I went over the mechanics of the journey sufficiently often to dispel worries. Rubberized cloth is the usual material for making balloons, but the price was prohibitive. Nylon-meshed plastic seemed potentially far stronger, and cheaper, too. And the plastic I chose seemed perfect.

The advantage of rubberized cloth over plastic is that it has a longer life and can easily be repaired if rips develop or small leaks show. From the manufacturer's angle this certainly has advantages, but as my journey was to be over the ocean, it seemed to me that such a precaution was almost as useless as the well-known parachute guarantee: "This article is guaranteed for life"—whose life?

My reinforced plastic bag was to be used once, then discarded. If I wished to make a second journey, then I could buy new plastic sacs fabricated specially for the chosen route and merely reuse the old rigging and equipment.

Balloon gas was a problem. Hydrogen was the obvious choice, and it is far from expensive—less than $300 for enough to fill my balloon—but the cost of transportation and deposits on the hydrogen cylinders would have cost me twenty times that much. Also, I did not know what rules and regulations concerning gas I could expect at the other side.

Other gases are used at times for lifting balloons. I took for granted that hot air was out of the question, for hot-air balloons of the latest type can stay aloft for only a few hours. Helium is another excellent gas, but this was much more expensive than hydrogen, and there were mechanical complications involved, in that the balloon would need to be much larger—and this in turn meant it would need to be structurally stronger. There were formidable export laws concerning helium also, and that ended any thought in that direction.

These and other problems I was examining when the Field Museum called.

"We asked for one dugout canoe from South America . . ." they said.

"You have a choice of two," I suggested.

". . . and we have chosen to keep the San Blas canoe," they went on.

So in the middle of winter I was given back the *Sierra Sagrada* minus the San Blas canoe.

It did not take me seconds to realize that the *Sierra Sagrada* would make an excellent transport for most of the parts of my proposed balloon crossing.

"I'll collect the *Sierra Sagrada* and take it around to Ralph Frese's Chicagoland Canoe Base by truck," I phoned.

The balloon transport problem had resolved itself, but the hydrogen problem remained. I checked the different alternatives and remembered a book that had been written about a highly patronized balloon journey in which the balloonists carried chemicals to make their own gas. This persuaded me that chemicals would be a practical way to generate my own hydrogen.

Cylinder hydrogen would be much too heavy for the *Sierra Sagrada* to carry. The weight of the lightest cylinders to carry sufficient gas for a 12,000-cubic-foot-capacity balloon was over 10,000 pounds, a weight that, added to the cost of the 58 cylinders that I considered necessary, made the problems seem insurmountable.

Chemical hydrogen was different. This ranged in price from sodium borohydride/cobalt chloride, which would have given me sufficient hydrogen, but it cost $22 dollars a pound. Plebeian calcium hydride, however, cost only $2.60 a pound, and one pound of calcium hydride would give me one pound of lifting capacity for my 600-pound balloon.

I ordered 600 pounds of calcium hydride and prepared a new design for a pontoon that would enable the *Sierra Sagrada* to take the extra weight. The chemicals were far too expensive for my depleted pocket: for one thing, I could not pay the apartment rent. But they were an essential part of the project, and, I asked myself, what is a month's rent compared with the prospect of a 3,000-mile balloon voyage across the Atlantic?

Once I had my balloon and chemicals, I decided I would have to wait until late spring before I could continue the *Sierra Sagrada*'s voyage. The Great Lakes and rivers freeze solidly in winter, and shipping lanes are not officially opened until April.

Canoeing of a different type was masterfully arranged by Ralph Frese. "Let's have a New Year's Break-the-Ice Party," he suggested. So, the first Sunday of the new year three 36-foot fiber-glass war canoes went chomping down the ice-encased Chicago River, loaded to the gunwales with genuine Indians, led by LeRoy Wesaw and Nathan Bird, and a couple of dozen paleface braves—blue-faced braves may be a more appropriate term, for the temperature hovered scarcely above the freezing point. It was tough on the paddles, since we had to break through one-inch-thick ice, icebreaker style, in order to make any progress.

John Hobgood, Barbara Tiritilli and myself proved to be such poor paddlers that we were excused from duty, and we huddled around a flask of rapidly vanishing brandy, wielding paddles only when we came to an especially thick section of ice.

It was an appropriate way to welcome in the new year.

Chicago's Adventurers Club had elected me a member, an honor that I was to appreciate more as time went along. Moral assistance is what I needed more than anything else, for I noted that my proposed balloon venture made many of my non-Adventurers Club friends nervous, and more than once I was entreated to stay with my feet planted on the sea-decks, or even on the land.

So many people proved to be jittery about the project that I kept my intentions confined only to the few people directly connected with the venture. I did not even tell Griffolyn Plastics, who manufactured the balloon, what the true purpose of the plastic was. A flat bag was what I asked for, and I explained in detail which edges should be sealed and which part could be left open. The original color was black, to preserve as much heat as possible—which in turn would allow me to reduce the hydrogen load.

I now set about making a new pontoon to replace the San Blas canoe. At first I considered building the pontoon in such a manner that it could double as a hydrogen generator, and I discussed the idea with some chemist friends. They were not too sure that the idea was feasible. They were concerned with the corrosive qualities of calcium hydroxide, while I was beginning to pay more attention to the heat involved.

Through the winter months I had ample time to ponder about these problems, for major construction work was halted by contrary weather. We had a tremendous snowfall in January, 1967, the greatest in Chicago's history. Buses came to a halt, cars were marooned, and city transportation was paralyzed for three days. It was great weather for photo-finishing, as everyone brought out cameras to take photographs of the great event, but not much use for anything else. Sliding and slipping on the snow-blocked streets, I concluded that standing solidly on the ground was not my main ambition.

"Rest is rust," old fishermen say, and I share the same opinion. For a month the Santa Marta hull lay under three feet of snow, as did the rigging, the connecting frame and the other parts of my equipment. Yet the snow was not an unmixed evil. As the snow thawed in February and March, my rigging was cleaned and overhauled. Even the termites in the mast finally had met their match; they had frozen in the bitter months.

By May my pontoon was nearing completion. Seamless lengths of sea-ply made the job easy, along with pre-cut lengths of four by four. What type of timber it was I neither knew nor cared; my concern was more with strength than with style. Again I relied on heavy, smooth-fitting joints, thoroughly caulked and sealed with boiling tar while dry. Neighbors closed their windows while I prepared the acrid brew. I ignored their justified complaints, and by the time I had finished the job, I knew the new *Sierra Sagrada* would withstand any sea. The North Atlantic can be tough at times, and it would not allow any short cuts.

The linked chains I had used the last time were discarded, and I made new supports at Ralph Frese's blacksmith shop. I hammered into shape two-inch by a quarter-inch pieces of mild steel over his anvil and secured them with five-eighths-inch bolts for tightening.

Ralph also suggested I use his workshop as a headquarters and mailbox, and this was the best idea of all, for my addresses were fragmented between work and apartment. Leon Siroto of the Field Museum prepared a list of things that would be of interest to the Museum should I venture inland from the African shore, and Austen Doe checked weather conditions that I would be likely to encounter on the way. New lists were formed, and I wrote to Johnson Motors to ask if the motor from my last year's journey was for sale, for it had behaved perfectly on the way up the Mississippi from Louisiana. "We'll send you a new one," they wrote back.

This offer was the turning point that told me that I finally was ready to begin the voyage. With the cash I had set aside for the motor, I now had sufficient funds to be on my way. So the final link in the order of preparation was forged. With all my equipment at hand, I set a sailing date for early June.

I was surprised at the number of people who had become involved and at the number of friends I had made: Ted

Wolfe, Art Myrland and Joe DeFillips of the Adventurers Club; Lois Lundy, my public relations girl at the Field Museum; Shirley McMillan of the Hektoen Institute; Bill Schaub of the Attorney General's office; Bruce Wolff, who had me elected an honorary member of the Lincoln Park Boat Club, from where I would launch the voyage; Inge Bredendieck; John Hobgood; Scotty Sumita; Dick Friedman, of course, the intrepid balloonist; and Austen Doe.

Going-away parties were the order of the day, until people started to ask when I was going away. But finally the end of May approached, and my June sailing date came closer.

Work had slowed down at La Salle Photofinishing, because after Easter many people laid aside their cameras until the summer. Bill Yamamoto knew of my plans to leave, and he would have been the last person to discourage my proposed journey.

Bill and I had a lot in common. Neither of us was scared to battle a little to get what we wanted. Bill and Grace had started their business from scratch after a number of setbacks and misjudgments. Now their turnover was more in a day than they used to earn in a year, and they were still expanding. Good luck, a good reputation and a lot of hard work had built a nucleus for Bill's photo-finishing laboratory, which I considered to be the best in Chicago.

"Single-handed voyage planned across the Atlantic," the headlines read. But I certainly did not feel as if I were going single-handed. Not with all these people involved!

One last party was given under a model of my square balloon. Inge and Gretchen had organized it. "You really want to make sure I go," I jested. We popped the cork of a champagne bottle and looked over a card Gretchen had written for the occasion.

*Good luck to Frank our sailor friend*
*Whose daring is quite rare.*
*You've sailed the seven seas before*
*Without a single care.*
*You plan a new adventure now*
*Of sailing through the air.*
*Please carry this in your valise*
*If you have room to spare.*

Spare room was at a premium on the *Sierra Sagrada*. But there was always room for a little more good luck!

I did not have a valise aboard, but a folding stationery and desk set in my filing system doubled as my ship's log. The good luck card was ceremoniously put inside and returned to Gretchen, a little water-stained maybe, when the *Sierra Sagrada* and I returned to Chicago 16 months later. The log, I realized then, was not much used; few details were written in it. Day-to-day routine was set down in my pocket diaries, as were the events surrounding the departure.

Frank Dallos helped me give the drums of calcium hydride a coat of fiber glass, and Dick Friedman and Austen Doe helped me with the final rigging. The Lincoln Park Boat Club provided facilities for launching, and June 6th was departure day. Austen volunteered to accompany me to Waukegan to meet John Tuzee and the Johnson Motor people.

After being given a rousing send-off by Nathan Bird's and Ralph's war canoes and by farewell honks of stationary launches, I headed into Lake Michigan.

Atlantic, here we come!

# Chapter VI

THE REDESIGNED *Sierra Sagrada* ran as smoothly and matronly as before. The old Cuna canoe had cut the water more easily, but the new pontoon was satisfactory. My most embarrassing items of cargo were the 18 drums of calcium hydride, which I estimated would be sufficient for the balloon journey across the Atlantic.

The balloon project was now officially known as Low Altitude Flying Feat, abbreviated to LAFF. This was by far the "tightest" journey I had ever attempted. Cash was short. I had no means of knowing what assistance or hindrance I would receive in Africa. One false move on my part, and the journey would be a failure. Operation LAFF was a realistic code name. It was also a realistic appraisal of my chances for success. I had taken every possible safety precaution: I could do no more.

The 22,000-cubic-foot-capacity balloon deflated into the front 16 feet of my canoe hold. This took a lot of valuable cabin space, but to its credit, if by chance the canoe were damaged, the buoyancy of the balloon sac alone would keep me afloat.

The chemical drums were originally supposed to fit lengthwise in my pontoon, and the original 22-foot length had had this in mind. But when I had coated the drums with fiber glass, I had found them too tight for comfort, and I also had been concerned that they would prove too difficult to inspect during the voyage. Rather than answer questions from the press in Chicago, I had stowed the chemical drums in my cabin, and when curious people looked inside the cabin, I had said they were food supplies. In fact, by departure time the inside of the *Sierra Sagrada* was so packed that not even I knew for sure what was in there.

In Waukegan, therefore, I took the chemicals out of the cabin again and chained the drums on deck, keeping 15 pounds of calcium hydride sealed separately in a plastic jar in case I chose to experiment en route. Austen took the Milwaukee Express back to Chicago, and I became acquainted with John Tuzee, of Johnson Motor's plant, and with some officials of Waukegan's civic administration who came to visit me while I transferred my cargo at the harbor front.

Making a boat shipshape takes time, and the *Sierra Sagrada* was no exception. Slowly I rearranged the cabin, until everything was enclosed in its own place and space. Heavy equipment, such as hammer, nails, spare anchor chain, saws and other tools, I stowed in the stern. A rack was made for lighter wrenches, files and screwdrivers. From a local store I purchased a new compass, which I secured in easy view in front of me on the cabin top. I also bought a supply of food to see me through the Great Lakes and generally prepared for the sheltered-waters stages of my journey.

Spoons, knives, forks, can opener, spare pocketknives and splicing pegs were classified as operating hardware and hung to port in my cabin. On the starboard were toiletries, such as mirror, razor, toothbrush, scissors, nail clippers and similar articles. Of all these things, I noted that the can opener was by far the most important item; without it the whole journey would have been in jeopardy.

The cabin walls were festooned with binoculars, spare compasses, face mask and snorkel, radio, watch and cameras; all hung on their own individual hooks, ready for instant use if the need arose. The two-inch-thick foam mattress that I had used from Colombia, which had required a plastic cover if I wanted it to act as a mattress and not as a sponge, had been replaced by a gaudy air mattress. Usually the weather was sufficiently agreeable for a light blanket only, but I was prepared for cold spells with a thick sleeping bag.

Food was kept in two large fishnet pockets secured to the hull amidships. More than 100 pounds of food could be stored in each of the pockets, but these were now flat and empty. I had no intention of buying bulk supplies until I reached my last port of call.

George Becker, a friend from my days in South America, had given me a .22 single-shot Savage—"To repel pirates," he said. George had taken my old 20-gauge shotgun last year when he had returned to the Mitu area in Colombia. The .22 I hung over my port-side food sacks. My twin-spring fish-spearing gun hung to starboard.

Every available inch of space was used. A narrow shelf in the forward part of the cabin held notebooks, spare film, fishhooks, medicines, pencils, passport and other small articles. A can with both ends cut out served as an excellent pigeonhole for my various charts. I even carried a typewriter, slung in a dry space in my mid-cabin section.

Considering that the maximum height of the cabin was 42 inches, I considered my stowing job to be excellent. "Surely you must have been cramped!" people have exclaimed. "Yes, at times," I'd admit, "but I have 26 feet of space when I'm empty in which to stretch." Even an eagle's nest is small, but that does not prevent the eagle from getting around. My cabin was only to sleep in; when not asleep, I wanted to be around, seeing what the land or the sea had to offer.

Ralph Frese had pasted "Keep Illinois Rivers Clean" stickers on my craft from stem to stern when it was being launched, for Ralph is an avid conservationist. In deference to his interest, I left the stickers on until I reached Two Rivers, but then I slipped them deep into the waters of Wisconsin.

Lake Michigan lived up to its usual irascible reputation, but the weather was good enough for me to average 50 miles a day. When setting sail, I followed the west coast, as protection from the winds, which usually prevail from the west. However, the winds were contrary and blew steadily from the east. As a result I made short-day's runs, especially since there was thick fog: Milwaukee to Sheboygan, Two Rivers to Kewaunee, and so on through the Sturgeon Bay passage. When I reached Clarence Reimer's marina in Marinette I loaded up with gasoline and started making longer hauls across the wider parts of Green Bay and the top part of Lake Michigan. And eventually my route led me to the Straits of Mackinac.

Although large ships reach the St. Lawrence River by way of the Great Lakes, a long and tedious trip over often treacherous waters, smaller craft can take a short cut through the sheltered waters of the Trent Canal, at the eastern extremity of Georgian Bay. The canal route cuts the distance in half, and I took it gladly.

Through locks and lakes the canal meanders. Once

this was war-whoop country. Ruthless Iroquois followed these same paths and waterways, making vicious raids on the agricultural and fishing Huron Indians. Samuel de Champlain followed this route when he discovered Lake Ontario in 1615 and is said to have led a band of retaliating Huron braves in a sneak raid against the Iroquois foes. Not for the first time I found myself wondering how it is that the Indians are never credited with discovering any part of the Americas. That's unfortunate for the Indians, but flattering to the British, French, early Americans, Spanish, Portuguese, and Leif Erikson and his Vikings. Nowadays the paint-streaked warriors with swaying headdresses of hawk and eagle feathers only emerge on July 4th and other visitor-saturated days. But the land is as wild as ever.

The Trent Canal was in flood after exceptionally heavy rains. The wooded slopes of the northern country still held back much of the rainfall, and the upper flood-control locks and gates were opened wide to prevent locally disastrous flooding. Along with the cascading water came logs, weeds and other flotsam and jetsam, which had accumulated during the previous fall in the northern tarns and waterways.

"You'll be traveling at your own risk," the lock-master at Port Severn warned me as I entered the canal's first lock and requested lockage to a higher level. I thought he was remarking about my boat, but he wasn't fooling. Two days later the authorities closed the lock completely, allowing no more vessels upstream.

The canal had some 43 locks, and at each stage I was told dire tales of how rough the next stage would be. There must have been at least three dozen large cruisers along the lock approaches, all heading for Lake Ontario. Many of the channel markers had been swept under the water's surface by the rapid current, so there was a valid reason for closing the canal—or almost valid, for I would not have appreciated being locked out.

Although the current was raging fast, the days were bright and sunny. Even the early morning fog usually had dissipated within an hour, and the heavy rains evidently had moved up to the higher river valleys. Two cruisers with which I traveled hit submerged channel-buoys and had to remain in Peterborough to replace their bent propeller shafts. The beauty of the *Sierra Sagrada* was that I could maneuver in my own length, thereby reducing the possibility of accidents to almost zero. To its credit, the Trent Canal is usually placid and is as pleasant a stretch of sailing ponds and small lakes as can be found anywhere.

Once more the combination of hot weather and fresh water brought out a crop of mushrooms along my hull. I call them mushrooms euphemistically, for to me they were just small brown lichens half an inch in diameter, and I was not sure if they were edible. I scrubbed the hulls down periodically, quite sure that the lichens would go away when I reached sea water.

Through the Thousand Islands I sailed, although my chart informed me there are really 1,246 islands there. Then I wound my way into the Upper St. Lawrence River. The Seaway locks were made for ocean ships, but so many pleasure craft were on their way to Montreal that the locks were always crowded. I did not tarry, but sailed on past Trois Rivieres and Quebec, to the place where the St. Lawrence gained gigantic dimensions and opened up till it was a mile wide.

Now I was in French Canada. Many of the small homes on the bleak river could easily have been imported from Brittany or Normandy. There were small crofters' *maisons* with slated roofs and tiny, frilly curtained windows, the inside of which had well-worn furniture and open fires.

I learned to ask for *essence* instead of gasoline, and I bought bread by the yard instead of by the pound. If I asked for anything in English, they would reply in French. And if I retaliated in my poor French, they would say, *"Mon Dieu,"* and try to remember their half-forgotten English.

Soon the river became tidal. The area between permanently flowing water and tidal seas is always choppy, especially during the period when the incoming tide is fighting against the outflowing current. In the St. Lawrence River these choppy waters lasted some 60 miles. Past Rimouski I was in open salt water and had to rely on carrying water flasks with me. Many times in the later parts of the journey I wished for the ice-cold refreshing water that I had drunk from the glistening rock-filled lakes of Georgian Bay and the nearby mountain-stream anchoring sites.

Fog was by far the biggest hazard as I traveled between the Gaspe Peninsula and the giant mid-channel island of Anticosti. An ocean-bound tanker loomed through the white-enveloping cloud 50 yards behind me, giving a deafening fog-hoot as it passed. I had not heard it approaching over the noise of my outboard motor. A startled crew member looked over the side as the *Sierra Sagrada* pitched and tossed as the bow wave swirled past. The stern of the tanker and its thrashing screw were lost in the fogged shroud before I was properly settled by the tiller and aimed for closer shore waters, and I wondered if the crew member was as shaken as I felt. With or without motor, fog is a frustrating thing. With my engine running, I could hear nothing coming. Without my engine running, I was virtually helpless before a ship's oncoming speed.

Just a few days previously I had been in five fathoms of water and had smelled the diesel fumes of a passing fishing vessel. But I still had not been able to see the craft. Nothing can be more nerve-wracking than hearing a ship's engines getting louder and not being able to see it or to know its direction. Only the passing bow wave and the fish-strong diesel smell had told me that the phantom craft had passed.

I found it safer to stay near the coast when fog was around or when it threatened. Later, in Newfoundland, I hugged the coast sometimes within 20 yards, guided by the white breaking waves of the shore. It was all too easy to stray out into the deep water.

The sail from Cape Gaspe to Newfoundland was across open gulf, and I could rely on the sail alone. It started off with a friendly wind but soon changed to a genuine pea-soup fog, which seemed even denser than usual. What looked like a dog's head appeared off my bow, and I steered across to rescue it. Then a second and third head appeared, and I saw that they were seals. Maybe they were as blind as I was, for I could see barely more than two boat lengths ahead.

The Labrador current flows strongly along the New-foundland coast, and I was pushed off course 60 miles north, landing in Lark Harbor, near Corner Brook.

Arctic ice has shaved the softer earth from Newfound-land's shore, and gray-shadowed cliffs and gale-smoothed rocks stretched and receded in my fog-restricted circle of vision as I groped along the shore seaward. I turned south to round Cape Ray's jagged headland toward Port-aux-Basques, and the waves had a longer and slower lilt as the Atlantic's force grew stronger. I was now through the Cabot

Strait, and the whole of the Atlantic lay open for thousands of miles to the south. Brazil would have been the first country I would have reached if I had headed that way. Even the color of the water somehow looked different, as though it knew its latent power.

This was no place to have weaknesses in any of my equipment, and I hove-to in Port-aux-Basques Harbor to check the rigging and straps. At the same time I hoisted a rotating radar reflector of carved aluminum sheet, to take advantage of any ships or craft that might have anti-collision radar.

The chemical drums were now being constantly soaked with water, and I noticed that the cap of one of the drums showed definite signs of bulging. With a great deal of apprehension I examined the fiber-glass covering, but a detailed examination showed the covering was flawless.

Then I realized that if there had been a flaw or a hole in the drum the gas would have escaped, and the drum would not have bulged. Obviously there had been water inside before the cans had been covered with fiber glass. Drilling a tiny hole in the bulging lid, I released the compressed hydrogen. When the gas had dissipated, I lit a candle and drooled dripping wax over the hole, sealing the drum securely for the remainder of the journey.

During my stay at Port-aux-Basques I was offered a crate of sardines at six cents a can. It was a good price, and I bought a couple of cases for my larder. Homemade bread was also for sale at all these ports, and I lived on sardine sandwiches during most of my Newfoundland passage.

After leaving Port-aux-Basques, I moved from one fishing hamlet to the next. Ever-friendly fishermen gave me lots of hints as I made my way eastward. Ocean currents are so strong around Newfoundland that one can ride them like giant escalators if he knows where the currents are, and I learned that the currents were practical roads to follow from island to island or from island to mainland. Along the coasts I sometimes gained two knots by following the local fishing community's directions, allowing me to reach towns that otherwise seemed too far away on the map. While making my first journey with the *Nengo*, I had used gasoline company road maps instead of charts. They had proved excellent and accurate, and I used the same idea this time. Judging by the few excursions I made to Newfoundland's interior, I think my choppy sea was smoother and easier than their rocky roads, although travelers on both were rare.

Some of the smaller communities did not even boast a road leading to them. One such town was Grey River, a mining and fishing settlement hemmed tight by a ravine of towering raw cliffs and devoid of anything growing except the smallest and hardiest of plants. Hardly more than a crack in the wave-surging seacliff led into a channel that was scarcely wide enough for the *Sierra Sagrada*.

Once past the breaking waves and rocks, the water lay serenely sheltered in a fiord. Bottle-fashion the fiord opened so that one minute I was clawing for space and the next I was in pond-smooth waters a full 200 yards wide. I tried to anchor against the sides, but the depth dropped like a cliff, and 20 fathoms of chain and rope failed to touch the bottom.

Motoring along the fiord for a further mile, I spotted Grey River settlement sitting on an isolated shelf-like niche behind an outjutting spur. The land covered no more than a square city block, surrounded by vertical slopes. Yet on this lonely land were built nearly 80 houses, and as the roar of my motor reverberated through the cliffs, heads popped out from 240 windows, or so it seemed. Then doors opened, and I swear everyone and everyone's pet was there to meet me when I arrived. Staying aboard ship in coastal towns was impossible. Grey River was no exception, and what it lacked in size, it made up in hospitality. The names of Newfoundland towns and villages often echo much of its sentiments and thought. Some of them are just mildly descriptive, such as Seal Cove, Hare Bay or Gull Island. Near the fishing grounds and cod banks are the more descriptive Fortune Bay and Despair Bay.

Newfoundlanders lead a hard life. The winter before I arrived the *Blue Mist* had been at sea in the bitter winter months with a full cargo of cod aboard. A raging gale and freezing weather had combined to cover the decks and rigging with spray, which instantly froze and accumulated until the ship was an ice-covered hulk, too heavy for her engines to move. Slowly she sat lower in the water. Within an hour the *Blue Mist* sank along with her crew. No one had a chance; even the lifeboats had frozen solid to the davits. A lot of work and danger goes into collecting cod in even the best months. In rain, fog or shine the harvesters of the sea go out daily, and during my stay in Newfoundland it was mostly fog.

When vision proved too restricted, I sheltered behind rocks and islands for the night. Many of the rocks were 40 feet high, so there was no shortage of shelter. Lulled by the quiet rolling boat, a good night's sleep was welcome at times.

One of my stipulations for sea journeys is an extra-long and extra-strong anchor and chain, with emphasis on the long length of chain rather than on a heavy anchor. In this way one can anchor out against the heaviest of seas and await favorable winds. I had 100 feet of three-eighths-inch chain plus 200 feet of rope—enough to anchor my 26-foot craft in almost any situation.

By making inquiries at Grey River, I learned that Trepassey Harbor would be the most favorable port for aiming across the Atlantic, for it lies at the most southeasterly part of Newfoundland. But first I wanted to visit St. Pierre. Thus leaving Grey River I headed in a southerly direction, first calling at Miquelon before continuing to the adjacent St. Pierre. St. Pierre and Miquelon are the last French possessions in North America, and many items available in their stores are duty-free. I had no stove aboard, so I loaded my craft with cognac and anisette. In terms of weight my new cargo certainly was no heavier than an alcohol stove, and it was also guaranteed to be 100 percent efficient. From the standpoint of calories, hot canned food and cold canned food are the same, and if a little cognac may not have added many calories, it certainly did not make the canned food taste any worse. "Cold coffee and hot beer" had been my only complaint on the *Sierra Sagrada* so far, and at least that little problem was taken care of for the present.

Cash had become embarrassingly short, and I sent away to my bank in Chicago to withdraw the few funds I had left. The overriding reason for making my journey as self-contained as possible was that I knew I would have no cash for anything except the barest essentials when I reached Africa. Everything I needed I intended to carry with me.

Aboard the *Sierra Sagrada* I had 80 copies of my book, *Long Sail to Haiti,* which had been published two years earlier and now was completely out of print. These I exchanged for gasoline and day-to-day provisions as I went along. I had used more than 500 gallons of gasoline reaching the Atlantic, and the income from the books was put to good use.

While waiting for my cash to arrive, I brought my correspondence under control. The limited space of the *Sierra Sagrada* did not allow fancy cabin space, and I am sure I had 5,000 tourists peering over my shoulder as I sat answering letters, typewriter on cabin top, with the wind blowing my papers away. With time to spare I retuned my motor and had my radio overhauled. Robert Gerignat, of the local meterological station, gave me hints for the best instruments for my forthcoming studies at sea, but these instruments proved too costly to afford, so I bought a few simpler, patented meters instead. I had not been keeping up my ship's diary, but now I prepared a weather log for use on the more serious stages of the journey.

By the time I was ready to leave St. Pierre, my cash from Chicago had still not arrived, but I made arrangements to collect it from a forwarding branch on the Newfoundland mainland. And, finally, early in August I headed for Trepassey, my last port of call. The inland and coastal journey was behind me.

# Chapter VII

Trepassey proved to be a small town. Fish products are its main source of income. Cod—fresh, cold, smoked and salted —keep the whole coast alive. The processing plant lay half a mile down-bay from my berth, and the *Sierra Sagrada* was tied to an auxiliary wharf alongside the workers' bunkhouse and cookhouse. I took advantage of their offer to fatten up with their home-baked meals.

We ate at a long-reach table. Plain solid biscuits, fish and potatoes were their mainstay; they were fishing folks and judged a dinner more by its size than by its looks. All along the southern coast of Newfoundland I found the same hospitality. "We do not have much to eat, but you are welcome to join us," they would say. Then they would serve a ten-inch platter piled so high you could lose your fork and half your elbow in it. Alongside they would have a warm plate of home-cooked biscuits to titillate the appetite further. Woe to anyone on a diet in Newfoundland!

My boat had that down-to-earth look of a craft built for a purpose. The brilliant red enamel had faded to a working color, and every item on deck was necessary. It would have been pleasant to have arrived on a more luxurious and spacious craft, but then I suspected that I might not have been so well received.

Repairing a leaking deck seam and completing the final overhaul of the outboard motor in preparation for the deep Atlantic kept me busy for six days. Eating, talking and selling copies of *Long Sail to Haiti* also combined to slow me down, for I would not be doing much of any of these activities while at sea, and I was making the most of my last opportunity. Selling my book became so successful, in fact, that my boat soon acquired the name *The Bookshop*.

One of my last days was spent on a quick taxi ride to St. John's to collect the cash forwarded to the bank there and to buy some final essential supplies, including weather equipment and a nautical almanac. Buses are almost non-existent among these isolated communities, and $10 for a round-trip ride of nearly 200 miles seemed a fair bargain. Francis O'Neil was the cabdriver, and we carried nine people in the six-seater both ways—which was the only way to make this a paying proposition.

Outfitting concluded, I made a final inspection. With pencil in hand I marked off the checklist of each and every item: chemical drums undamaged and secure; balloon plastic fitting tight in the Santa Marta hull; motor running smoothly and greased; anchor chain and rope coiled and unfrayed; canoe-straps firm; mast and rigging secure and tight; sails ready for immediate use; stores packed; compass zeroed; kayak secured. I had brought a fiber-glass kayak with me, a brilliantly red-colored object, which I lashed on deck between the hulls as a possible dinghy. A secondary use for the dinghy was as a life raft for the balloon journey, an idea I later discarded in favor of an inflatable rubber boat.

There were a few other things I would have liked to have done, but both cash and time were at a premium. It would have been pleasant, for example, to have invested in a new radio or to have motored to St. John's to dry-dock and repaint. All journeys can be improved, and I was already a week overdue. The weather was in my favor now, and this made me determined to sail as soon as possible. If I waited too long, I could easily run into fall storms.

"Tomorrow morning I sail," I told John McGrath, a fish-research skipper at the same cannery-quay.

"Good idea. We don't often get weather like this," was his only comment.

John had sailed northern waters from Europe to West Canada, in everything from three-masted sailing ships to his present modern vessel, the *Oderin*, and he could sense the next day's weather equally as well as anyone along the coast.

Now that the prospect of the sea journey was upon me I had the urge to savor the firmness of dry land, for once I sailed I would be seeing nothing but the sea for a month or more. With a small knapsack swinging by my side, I walked up the winding harbor road and turned off at a windswept rocky path toward a distant peak. There was nothing along the bay but a deserted shepherd's hut and a couple of stunted pine trees. Trepassey is a desolate area, but, in a wild and unbridled form, it is reminiscent of the Scottish Highlands.

I walked for a couple of hours along meandering paths amid gauze-like scrub. A fine drizzle of rain, scarcely more than a mist, hid the lower harbor from sight. Whenever the paths forked, I chose the path that seemed to lead upward. Water level is what I wanted to escape, if only for a few hours. The walk cleaned my system. I did not wish to speak to anyone or even to see anyone. I just wished to be left alone with my thoughts and to devour the last feel of land.

It was dark when I returned to Trepassey, and the tiny town was asleep. I sat leaning against the cabin, listening to the radio for a couple of hours, before I, too, turned in for the night. It was my last night in still waters, and I slept soundly. The morning of August 15th was bleak and thick with dew when I awoke—the type of morning to which I had become accustomed all along the Newfoundland coast.

I stirred myself and checked the decks before slackening my mooring lines. Along the bay a masthead-light bobbed, and I saw that I was not alone. Probably he was an early worker at the canning factory, for he was heading in that direction. It was time for me to be going also, and as my motor roared to life I set the controls on troll and eased myself out of the harbor.

There was no one at the quay to see me go, for the town would not be awake for another hour or more. Once I cleared the Trepassey capes and shallows, it was a clear run to the open sea. Five-fathom swells kept the sea choppy at first, but they smoothed as the sea grew deeper. Rather than fight the westerly counterdrift of the Newfoundland current, I motored south-by-east at half-throttle. This would take me to the flowing edge of the cross-Atlantic gulf stream.

It was a chilly morning, so I wrapped myself in my parka and hoped that the dawn would break brighter as the sun climbed. Warm waters from Florida's gulf stream join the frigid flow from the Arctic north, causing morning fogs so thick that they make the river pea-soupers look like bouillon by comparison. I was told that 20 miles offshore, where the waters were more temperate, there was a 50–50 chance of clear skies. The hours passed briskly, and the first cold seas cascaded amidships as the vast ocean assumed command. Now I would have to rely on the fickle Atlantic with its fickle weather—something over which I had no control.

I breakfasted lightly and steered as favorably to my chosen course as the sea permitted. Thousands of gannets wheeled overhead, and chubby puffins swam alongside and under the bow, making me fear that I would hit them with the screw of my outboard motor. But these and other land-based birds I soon left behind. I spotted a solitary seal ten miles out to sea, and a lone seagull followed me until well into the evening. Then I was on my own.

As the fog and the day grew lighter, I passed a line of ships plying the St. Lawrence River route to and from Europe. I was pleased that none of them came close, for I doubted if my craft looked very seaworthy.

I had 48 gallons of gasoline lashed on deck, of which 24 gallons were earmarked for the outbound part of my voyage, and 24 to reach the next port. In between, I would sail.

There were two main projects I wished to study on the journey: how much fresh water is necessary on any given sea journey; and some new navigational ideas. On both of these projects I had pet theories that I would put into practice before the journey was through.

Both of my experiments seemed adequately insured. I had five gallons of fresh water lashed on deck plus liquid in all the cans of food I had on board. For navigation I had an alarm clock, a pocket watch, my rather battered transistor radio and a copy of Brown's *Nautical Almanac*. In Chicago I had bought a $60 automatic wristwatch, but it had broken before I had even left the city, and presumably

was still at the manufacturer's southside repair shop. As I
headed out to sea my only concern was that this would be an
easy and boring journey.

A following sea with a six-foot swell scudded me along.
True to prediction, the sky cleared after six hours of motoring, leaving above me a cloudless blue sky. Periodically, I
dropped a thermometer over the side as I maintained a
southeast bearing, watching as the water temperature rose
from under the 50-degree mark until it reached a steady 62
degrees Fahrenheit—the temperature of the gulf stream.

However, I found that I had to use the remainder of the
24 gallons of gasoline, for I was already overloaded and
could not afford to carry the extra weight. With the sea
behind me I plodded ahead at full throttle, until the final
tank hiccoughed to a halt at 6:45 P.M. Now I was a sailboat
again.

There were a few final points to attend to before I
hoisted sail. I had only four gauged motor-tanks from
Johnson Motors, and as these were now empty, I refilled
them from my four auxiliary six-gallon gasoline drums. I
then sealed the motor with canvas and plastic, to prevent it
from being constantly soaked with sea-spray. Last, but not
least, I lashed amidships the anchor and chain to prevent
them from being swirled overboard in any rough seas. With
everything properly secured, I hoisted sail with a steady
west wind filling my canvas, stretching my rigging just
enough for the *Sierra Sagrada* to squeak in contentment.

Leaving the mizzen furled, I made headway under
mainsail and jib. The *Sierra Sagrada* reacted favorably.
With the tiller lashed, I could walk on deck instead of being
enslaved in the cockpit. My rubber-soled shoes were slip-
pery, and I stripped to socks, pushing my shoes into the
overlaying plastic of the balloon in the forward hold. An

unexpected thrill of freedom ran through me as I looked around and saw nothing but open seas and dancing waves. Even the harshness of the motor, invaluable though it had been, had reminded me too vividly of scheduled routes and stops.

Sails are free as the wind. A sailor keeps one eye on the horizon for winds to help him or for breaking seas that he must challenge—or sometimes a little of both. It was very satisfactory. No cars. No pavements. Not even taxation to worry about until I returned. Instead of being tense at the start of the trip, I actually started to unbend and relax.

Sea-breezes are certainly free, but they are also cool at times. Before nine o'clock that night I reefed sail to two jibs only, and after a final check around the decks went into the sheltered cabin for a good night's rest. *"Only a crazy man paddles downstream,"* the Malays say, and I was relying on the trans-Atlantic current to help me along at a steady 12 miles a day.

On the second day out I was buzzed by the Russian trawler *Froznoft*. If bureaucracy has a sense of humor, the Russian ship's name could be an abbreviation for *fro*zen *north fleet*. Probably the crew had heard of my departure over the Newfoundland radio. I like Russians. They can be the most hospitable people in the world. During many a train journey in the Balkan States I have ironed out the bumps on the road with them, while sharing black bread and vodka.

The *Froznoft* cut her speed to my two knots and ran within 60 feet of my outrigger. All the crew seemed to be on deck, and each member seemed to have a camera in his hand. At such a speed the trawler would have little control, and I hoped that whoever was on the wheel kept his eye on the sea ahead.

A deckhand at the ship's bow threw a heaving line across my rigging. It was less complicated to cooperate than to try to get away. Attached to the heaving line was a large plastic bag, with a second plastic bag holding a couple of loaves of bread and three cans of fish in tomato sauce (price: 61 kopeks each). A note with the loaves read "HAVE A GOOD VOYAGE! GOOD LUCK! 15. 08. 67. CREW OF FROZ-NOFT." It was a nice gesture. I just wished they had thought to include some vodka.

The northwesterly wind changed to southwest, remaining there during most of my journey across the Atlantic. If my navigation instruments had remained intact, I would have been able to use it to take me to the Azores perfectly. However, these were to be put out of commission in a few days, and I was unable to steer with such accuracy.

My radio was first to go. It had already endured two of my South American expeditions, and I should have suspected its ability to take any more abuse. Although the Atlantic is usually kind to small craft, it is notoriously tough on equipment. Shortwave radio stations, which should have been loud and clear, were now so weak that I often could not find them. From about the sixth day out, most of my time was guesswork. What further griped me was that I had known that I would have to buy a new set at my first port of call, and its collapse within a week meant that my false economy had boomeranged.

When the sun shone, I hung the radio in the rigging, and sometimes it dried sufficiently to get 15 or 20 minutes' reception. At least, its failure was a perfect example of how humidity affects everything at sea.

Two subjects are frequently discussed among seafaring people: *the difficulty of keeping anything dry on small boats,* and, *the danger of being lost at sea without drinking water.*

I have always thought that surely there must be some relationship between these two diametrically opposite points. Too much dampness to keep dry; not enough water to drink. There must be a simple way to change humidity to fresh water. What the method is, I do not know, although I maintain that if you keep your clothes thoroughly wet night and day, then no body fluids will be lost through the skin pores.

All of us who have soaked in a hot bathtub for half an hour or have washed dishes for a similar length of time have noticed how the skin grows thick and soft. This is osmosis: water has penetrated through the skin in a reverse-to-normal direction. High humidity collects between waves, especially in turbulent waters such as the Atlantic's. Lungs must be wet to work efficiently. Breathing in the high humidity and spray will keep the lungs moist, and in such conditions, I believe, the lungs' humidity cannot fall below 100 percent. And finally, it seems to me, if the lungs and throat are saturated with humidity, then there is only one way that the moisture can trickle: down to the lungs and the stomach, making a reservoir.

Thus a combination of wet clothes and high humidity would probably enable a person to cross the Atlantic without *any* drinking water, although I prefer to play safe by saying that a combination of wet clothes and high humidity can cut down water needs by 90 percent of normal requirements.

The water requirements of different people, at different times, under different weather conditions vary so much that exact figures would be meaningless. I could probably cross the Atlantic without a drop of water—which would be uncomfortable and dangerous. It would definitely not do my health any good, and I would be so prepared in advance that it would hold no validity as a survival test.

However, I had hoped to find a way to change humidity to fresh water mechanically on the journey, but I remained as baffled as ever. Possibly a difference in temperature is the main ingredient.

One of my main occupations while sailing along was to inflate plastic bags; leave plastic bags in other plastic bags; tow plastic bags behind me; weigh plastic bags ten feet in the ocean; leave crumpled pieces of plastic sheet on relatively dry parts of the boat's rigging; and hang long plastic strips from various lines and halyards. But I never managed to condense sufficient water to warrant further tests.

On my taxi ride to St. John's I had bought an inexpensive humidity meter and three thermometers, to take readings of the humidity index at different heights above the deck. But the humidity meter rusted solid, and a more practical way proved to be simply to look at the state of the sails or rigging. Sometimes I would leave my sleeping bag or clothes to dry, and they would refuse to dry one iota from sunrise to sunset. Other times a frost-white layer of salt would appear within minutes, and everything was soon salt water soaked.

Clothes-drying was a more practical way of estimating the humidity than all the fancy meters in the world. The cabin was never dry. Nor did I want it too dry, for a dry wood boat is a wet wood boat in the first gale. But I must say it shook me a little when my friends the mushrooms started growing on the inside of the hull. But I supposed that if the mushroom spores were on the outside, there was no reason that they should not be on the inside. It reinforced my humidity-evaporation idea just fine, but I would have preferred their not being there. They seemed out of place.

Still, I was not hungry enough yet to eat them, so I let them grow in comfort.

Meals were simple affairs. A can opener gave me either beans or spaghetti. Chocolate bars, dates and hard candy were snacks I munched for the first 30 days, until it became apparent this was going to be a longer journey than I had anticipated. A few cans of meat supplemented my diet, and a couple of bottles of tomato sauce and the large supply of sardines helped disguise the sameness of my fare.

A short time after leaving Newfoundland, I went forward to refill a bottle with fresh water from the container lashed on the deck forward of my cabin and found that the mainsail-line had chafed a hole through its plastic side. I had lost three gallons of water; the remainder of the water in the container was salty and undrinkable. In practice, I was not overconcerned. Not being a lover of even 65-degree fresh winds, I was always swathed in half a dozen layers of clothing plus a heavy parka. Water splashes and having to go forward over the ever-awash deck kept my clothes wet most of the time and made it almost impossible to dehydrate.

However, catching rainwater was now added to my daily tasks. But collecting rainwater and sailing are incompatible tasks. It was either one or the other. To sail was to make the most use of the wind, and to collect water was to bring the sails into as calm a position as possible, and yet the rain always brought with it a high wind.

I found out early that rainwater caught as it dripped from the sails was so salty as to be unpalatable and that laying out too large a sheet of plastic to collect water defeated its own purpose, since the water collected was always ruined by flying salt-spray. So I evolved the slow process of laying a small sheet of plastic over the sliding hatch-cover.

This I could protect from sea-spray with my raincoat, and although small, the water it collected was drinkable.

Sometimes I had problems. On the 14th day out a heavy drizzle fell, the first in days. With the plastic sheet in front of me, I ladled the accumulating water spoonful by spoonful into an open-necked coffee jar and within 40 minutes had collected a full quart of water. Still the drizzle came, and I was reluctant to let it pass uncollected. Next I filled a large enamel drinking mug, and when this also was filled, I transferred the water to an empty Chianti bottle. However, since the bottle was round-bottomed, it was difficult to sit or lean against anything on deck, and rather than open the cabin-hatch I hooked the bottle by a string to a jib-cleat and left it dangling over the side.

Suddenly, with a freshening of the wind, the *Sierra Sagrada* gave a lurch, and the taut string slipped past the smooth top of the hanging Chianti bottle's neck. The bottle sank straight as a stone into the sea before I had time to grab it. Never have I sworn at a bottle so thoroughly, especially at a full one. To make things worse the rain had stopped, and I was left with only the original coffee jar of water. The wind blew harder, and I sat soaked to the skin with drizzle and spray, disgusted with the world in general and cursing the whole Italian nation for producing such a contrary shaped bottle.

Albatross were always around, sometimes as many as 50 at a time. They were not the great lone albatross of Ancient Mariner fame; these were small birds with brown backs and scrubby white bellies. They were forever squawking and squabbling with each other, and their main enjoyment seemed to be to fly alongside the glassy side of breaking waves, window-shopping for small fish. At night, when I left my Coleman lamp burning, the birds made pests of themselves by constantly fluttering into my sails or rigging. At times I was not sure if peace and quiet would not be better than the security of a light at night.

Shearwaters also liked the light. In daytime they zoomed between the valleys of the waves, but at night they settled in the sheltered lee of my cabin's side, looking like miniature black ducklings.

On August 29th I was surprised to see a pair of large turtles swim by. They were being harassed by green dolphins, the same as I had seen in the Caribbean, and if I had had a stove aboard, I might have taken advantage of their predicament and heaved them aboard for dinner.

I was off the main trade routes. My pilot-chart showed that most ships would pass north of me, following the shortest arcs of navigation.

I was in one of the freak currents that flows north from Florida and the Bahamas, taking isolated tropic seas halfway to the arctic circle. Since the water temperature had reached 74 degrees. I decided to take the opportunity for a quick swim to check the condition of my hulls under water. In Newfoundland I had intended to do the same, but the water was far too cold for me to summon up sufficient courage.

I lowered the sails and searched through the cluttered gear of my cabin until I had located my diving mask and snorkel, and within minutes I was taking my first swim of the Atlantic section of my journey. I found that my hulls were clean and the straps fitted snugly, but I felt uneasy in the water and was soon on deck and into my clothes again. There were too many sharks in the water, and I had not forgotten the meeting I had with the five-foot shark in the Gulf of Mexico.

In 1966, a journalist named David Johnston and a

public relations man named John Hoare had tried rowing across the Atlantic from the East Coast of the United States to Europe in an open boat called the *Puffin*. They never made it. The boat was later found drifting right-side-up but empty; of the rowers there was no sign. Very probably one of the pair had gotten in trouble, and his companion had swam after him to help; sharks may well have been the trouble here. Two others rowed across the Atlantic at almost the same time, on a similar route, but they were successful.

Portuguese men-of-war and Sargasso weed soon became common. Small fish that had made a home for themselves under the shade of my hull were delighted with the Sargasso. Out they darted to forage and pounce on the sea-lice and crustaceans that clung and lived in the Sargasso patches.

Sometimes an exodus occurred in the other direction. Crabs that had grown too large to dwell in the Sargasso weed sidled across to plant themselves along the iron straps that held the *Sierra Sagrada*'s hulls in place and, I suspected as the weeks went by, among the barnacles that had taken hold. As for the Portuguese men-of-war: What enemies can they have that would care to swallow the yards of stinging tentacles they trail below?

Gradually my food supplies were depleted, for I normally have a healthy appetite. But at least I was able to throw overboard the empty boxes that still littered my food sacks, and the *Sierra Sagrada* began to look shipshape again. Typewriter and clothes were stowed in their respective plastic bags. Sometimes I tried my hand at fishing but watching a fishing line usually bores me. Even more important, weather clouds were starting to build up, and I suspected we were soon going to have turbulent weather.

# Chapter VIII

THE FREAK warm current faded. Within a couple of days the sea temperature dropped to 68 degrees, and the air showed an even bleaker 55 degrees. Choppy seas prevailed, and white-capped waves that broke from all directions became a constant source of trouble. The tiller took the brunt of the force, but I had to steer every minute that I wanted to make headway.

On September 3rd (my 19th day) I got it in the neck, figuratively and literally. It was nearing sundown and all afternoon the sea had been choppy. Suddenly, the wind strengthened, as is its usual manner at sundown. I heard a roar behind me as waves broke. "Here comes another dumper," I thought, for they had been coming all day. A cavity formed under my stern, slowly going forward until it seemed to reach three parts to my bow. I slid backward. "This is going to be a big one," I almost had time to say. Glancing back, a wall of green water was piling high above me. I braced myself but was thrown forward like a rag doll as a mountainous sheet dropped on my back, leaving me soaking wet, breathless and spluttering. In addition, there were eight inches of water in my cabin and a broken rudder hammering against my stern.

The *Sierra Sagrada* groaned for minutes in a bubbling sea of foam. I hardly knew what to tackle first, but I slackened the sail halyards cautiously before making a more detailed check. The rudder was in two separate pieces, and the lower part was threatening to tear away in the swirling current.

It is fortunate that the tiller was easily unhooked. Tying rope-loops through each of the iron rudder-brackets, I removed the rudder pivot-pin and soon had the broken rudder lashed securely on deck. Then I dropped the sails and bailed for 30 minutes. My clock and radio were ruined; my bedding and clothes soaked. To complete the chaos, I had broken the glass of the Coleman lamp while heaving the rudder parts aboard.

At first I tried to relocate the floating cans and pencils and scraps of paper that hung soggily around the freshly bailed cabin, but soon I said, "To hell with it." The clothes in my plastic bag were still dry, and I still had most of a bottle of brandy left and a couple of mouthfuls of schnapps. If ever a person needed warming, it was I.

Morning broke no brighter than the night before. I only remember staring moodily around as I waited for my clothes and bedding to dry, wishing that I had something else in the bottles to tide me over.

Fixing a rudder at sea is no fun, but the weather-helm was too great for me to sail without it. The small surface area of my sails was insufficient to overcome the large surface area of my canoes, plus my kayak, plus my chemical and gasoline drums combined with the weight of my balloon and the stores. I drifted sideways, trying vainly to bring my bow or sails into the wind.

I had a lot more equipment than I had originally planned for in Cartagena, Colombia. The sail then had been planned for two almost empty canoes. Now I had 1,500 pounds of extra cargo, most of it on my Santa Marta canoe alone. Combined with my now water-soaked canoes, this meant a three-inch deeper load line, and every extra gallon of water that has to be pushed to one side needs or uses that much extra amount of power.

The *Sierra Sagrada* was as safe as ever, but even before the rudder broke she was nowhere near as maneuverable. More sail area and a new rudder would have made ideal additions. But then, so would have more time, more cash and many more other things, but nothing would be gained by worrying about that now.

Again I tried to sail without the rudder, and again the *Sierra Sagrada* broached or rode only slightly into the wind before falling off entirely out of control. An abandoned idea I had had in Canada was a false-bow guard for my outrigger. I had bought one-inch planks and lengths of five-sixteenth-inch running thread to hold the parts together. These materials now served a more useful purpose.

A patchwork job would have been a waste of time, so I took the rudder apart, drilled new holes to brace the strengthening planks and hoped that the newly constituted whole was as strong as it had been before. By September 6th the rudder was once more in place, and I was sailing steadily east-by-south. I took the belated precaution of putting wooden block-wedges in front of the hatch-slide so that pooping-seas could fall on me but not roar through the cabin.

Although the *Sierra Sagrada* was as strong as ever, my navigation equipment was completely ruined. All I had to rely upon was Brown's *Nautical Almanac* and a pocket watch that fluctuated wildly, sometimes losing ten minutes a day and other times stopping completely.

Time is *the* crucial element in navigation. I had all the time in the world, but what I needed most was to know accurate Greenwich mean time. If I know the length of the day or the length of the night, then by checking with the appropriate tables in my almanac I can estimate my latitude. If I know Greenwich mean time, I can compute longitude.

During the summer months, the length of the day in many parts of the northern hemisphere lasts 16 hours or longer. On the equator the length of the day always hovers around the 12-hour mark. In Philadelphia or Denver, for instance, which are both on the 40° north latitude, the time between sunrise and sunset each June 21st is 15 hours, 01 minutes long. Places on the 45° north parallel, such as Minneapolis or Yellowstone National Park, enjoy 15 hours, 37 minutes on the same day. The formula is simple and well known: the further north one goes in summer, the longer the length of the day.

However, in the northern hemisphere, and in the southern, too, for that matter, the length of the day and night are almost identical at the time of the spring equinox and of the autumn equinox: 12 hours each. Spring equinox is March 21st; autumn equinox is September 21st. I was nearing the September 21st equinox, so that the length of the day varied almost not at all, regardless of whether it was north or south.

I made a table:

|  | Latitude | Sunrise | Sunset | Length of day |
|---|---|---|---|---|
| Sept.<br>21st | 56° North | 0546 | 1758 | 12 hrs. 12 min. |
|  | 40° North | 0548 | 1757 | 12 hrs. 09 min. |
|  | 40° South | 0548 | 1758 | 12 hrs. 10 min. |
|  | Latitude | Sunrise | Sunset | Length of day |
| June<br>21st | 56° North | 0313 | 2050 | 17 hrs. 37 min. |
|  | 45° North | 0413 | 1950 | 15 hrs. 37 min. |
|  | 40° North | 0431 | 1932 | 15 hrs. 01 min. |
|  | 56° South | 0933 | 1530 | 5 hrs. 57 min. |

When I lost my radio and clock, I was near the 40° north parallel, but since it was September, I needed accurate time almost to the second to tell me my latitude. If it had been the middle of June, as the tables show, there would have been at least seven minutes longer between sunrise and sunset for each degree of latitude I was north of 40° north. With such a time difference I could even have used my cantankerous pocket watch and still have obtained a fair amount of accuracy.

To get away from figures and back to the *Sierra Sagrada:* I soon had no idea where I was. All I knew was that I was lost somewhere in the North Atlantic Ocean and that I ought to buy a more substantial radio at my earliest opportunity.

Rather than risk drifting south into the Doldrums, I made a new course as easterly as possible. The cabin of the *Sierra Sagrada* was once more dry and cozy, and any frayed worries I may have had over the last turbulent days were soon forgotten.

Whole armadas had sailed the seas in safety for centuries without radios and wristwatches. It was probable that half the world was discovered this way. It was also probable that I would reach the Azores if I kept on an easterly course.

Each day passed in much the same way. I would awaken at first light, usually some 30 minutes before sunrise. If the pocket watch was ticking, I would make an estimate of the time of sunrise and note it in my log. Fully half the time clouds were thick, so the estimate was vague, and fully half the time the pocket watch had stopped. Never did I miss a transistor more.

A full moon would sometimes fool me into rising an hour early, for full moon is always opposite the sun and so would be setting in the west about the same time the sun was about to break over the horizon in the east. Many times an undimmed full moon would have more light than a cloud-covered sunrise.

One annoying feature about the *Sierra Sagrada* was that there were no windows or glass ports. Hail, rain, or shine— if I wished to see what conditions lay in store, then I would have to rise and poke my head out of the hatch.

After sunrise had passed, I had a canned breakfast, usually of sardines and biscuits, or of sardines and beans when my supply of biscuits was gone. Within the hour I would clean my teeth and rub a salt-water-soaked facecloth in a cat-lick wash. Then I would repair rips in my sailing clothes or sails and in general would tidy the craft and check the rigging.

At first I tried to trim my ferocious beard and shave my sideburns a little, but my razor blades rusted into wafers, and my scissors snapped in two while serving the double purpose of cutting canvas squares to reinforce the sails. Eventually even the silver backing leached off my mirror, and it lay in disuse in the hold.

This was the wettest journey I was ever on. Almost everything that couldn't rust came apart at the seams. If it was made of aluminum, it grew little carbuncles and powdered away to a soft white dust. Plastic alone was immune. The wood of the dugout canoe also remained unscathed.

Middays and afternoons were spent at the tiller, and every minute I was at the tiller I tried to gain every inch of speed possible. Each wave that came along I checked, hoping that I could use its thrust to move me faster or in a more southeasterly direction. It was becoming rapidly apparent that the southwest wind combined with the current was pushing me northward at an alarming rate. But how much I was drifting I could not discern in the turbulent seas.

Sometimes ships passed close at hand. Twice I must have been seen or distinguished on radar, but both times I was left alone. One of the ships found me in the daytime, when the wind was straight from my bow and I was marking time with my mizzen streaming and all my other sails down. The wind prevailing against the current made the sea violent and choppy, and I was bouncing like a cork. Even for a ship of the size of the one that came to investigate me, the weather was rough, and I waved an O.K. sign as one of the officers checked with binoculars from the ship's bridge.

The other ship came at night. It circled me, and I was in a quandary whether to show a light and risk being misunderstood or to remain unlit and hope they would go away. I remained unlit, and they did go away.

I was not ungrateful to these ships. From the 19th day to well into the 30th day I was still certain I would reach the Azores as planned. But as the 40th day approached, I began to suspect that I had overshot my mark.

On September 28th, my 44th day, the navigator of the *Hornsee* confirmed my suspicions. I was 45° 22′ north and 20° 45′ west. The island of Flores, my Azores target, was 39° 30′ north and 31° 30′ west. I had overshot my mark by 600 miles. That is an awfully long way to go wrong and an even longer distance to make up.

I flagged the *Hornsee* down on the spur of the moment. It was early evening, not too dark, and the sea was pleasantly easy; I was sitting at the tiller without paying any particular attention to anything. Even above the sea's constant roar a ship's engines can be heard from far away. The night was fair, and, looking back, I could see a cargo-passenger ship on a passing course some 800 yards away. I doubted if they could see me in the dusk. It was the *Hornsee*.

When I was leaving Chicago, a sales-promoter had donated two flashing safety-flashlights—the type used on the side of a car if it stops for emergencies on the highway at night. One of these I had given to Austen Doe. The other I had kept. Now it was used for its original purpose. As the *Hornsee* passed, I flashed the light, and—good sailors as most ship's captains are—the *Hornsee* stopped for me.

The steering was perfect. Stopping engines to windward, the captain maneuvered his ship until I was in its lee and cradled against the *Hornsee's* side. Dropping fenders and a ship's ladder over the side, the captain invited me aboard.

Captain Schroder greeted me jovially: "You are getting dangerously close to shore."

"What shore?" I wanted to know.

It seems that I was well on my way to Europe.

Two matelots scrambled down to the *Sierra Sagrada* to save her from being pounded against the *Hornsee*'s iron sides. Although the Atlantic was smooth by usual standards, it still had a rolling swell of eight to ten feet.

We went up a flight of stairs to the navigation room. My position showed 700 miles from Portugal and 800 miles from Ireland. If I was not careful, I was going to miss Africa completely. What navigation!

The *Hornsee* seemed to be rolling all over the ocean. I weaved after the officers to the saloon, clinging to supports all the way. This was landsickness. Forty-four days at sea on my small boat had fooled my balance mechanism into thinking that all the world normally gyrated like a cork in a washing machine, a feeling that was to be even more pronounced when I finished my crossing on the *Kostroma* after 106 days.

I must have looked hangdog dry, for I had exhausted my spare water supply the day before.

"What can we get you?" I was asked.

I chose lemonade, and it was not the weak bubble-water hardly strong enough to pour from cans, but a robust German lemonade, made from almost undiluted lemons. It was hardly surprising that I was starting my second bottle before the first had time to settle in my stomach.

Chief Mate Schuldt told me that he had been on watch when the light flashed and that he had wasted no time ringing down to First Engineer Oltmanns to stop the engines. But perhaps we should let Alex Oltmanns tell how we met, somewhere in the middle of the rolling Atlantic Ocean.

# Chapter IX

It was around 1900 hours shiptime, corresponding to 2200 hours Greenwich mean time. Captain Schroder and I sat in the cabin. Prophetically, we were discussing things that could happen in the near future—nothing definite, just generalizations. I've forgotten the exact subject, but I remember that we were in general agreement.

The weather was quiet. We motored moderately at normal speed in the direction of the English Channel; Le Havre would be our next port. And I knew in advance we would have to wait for the morning's high tide before entering Le Havre basin, so there was no haste or urgency. But we had two more days of travel before we needed to concern ourselves with Le Havre.

Our cozy chat was disturbed by a telephone call. On the other end of the line Chief Mate Schuldt asked for the captain. Schuldt's voice had an urgent ring, and I wasted no time passing the phone across the table. "What is it?" I thought. It could not be the weather, surely.

I could just barely hear the voices. A light had been sighted momentarily from the bridge, and in the fading dusk Chief Mate Schuldt thought he had spotted a sail.

"Signal for full-astern, and use your judgment until I

get there," ordered Captain Schroder, and he slammed
down the phone and made his way to the bridge.

"Should I switch to diesel or rely on engine oil?" It
bothered me even as I made my way down. This was my
department and I would have to make the decision. Normally we ran with heavy crude oil. However, for emergencies
and fast maneuvering, such as when docking and in narrow
channels, we use diesel oil for its added dependability.

Switching from hot and heavy engine oil to cold diesel
is an acceptable way to stop the engines slowly. This seemed
to be such an emergency, and I valved the lines across.
Hardly was the diesel flowing than "Machine, Attention"
sounded over the telegraph. This was followed by "Half-
speed" and then "Stop."

The emergency maneuver seemed to have passed, but
everything was still prepared for a fast start if necessary.
There was nothing further I could do, so I handed over
again to the motor crew and went on deck to see what lay
up there.

On the bridge, in the meantime, neither Captain Schroder
nor Chief Mate Schuldt could see anything other than darkness. All the bridge lights had been extinguished to get
greater visibility, and they searched the seas for any sign
of a light or movement. Chief Mate Schuldt explained
what he saw, or thought he saw, and the steersman did
the same.

Then from the stern the light came again. Then it vanished. There was certainly something there. Then on and off
the light started flashing brightly, and it was definitely sig-
naling.

Captain Schroder issued the commands that steered the
*Hornsee* to windward of the flashing light. When the exact
spot he wished was reached, he ordered, "Half-speed," then,
"Halt."

As I reached the deck, Captain Schroder was descending
from the bridge. The ship's rail was already crowded with

curious passengers and crew. In the lee, close to, I could see a most unusual vessel. With a flat deck and low masts, it looked almost like a raft. I found out later it was two canoes, one decked and the other used as an outrigger, with a very low-rigged sail.

"What can we do for you?" we shouted. An odd greeting, I thought later, but we had to shout something.

"All I want is . . . " was all we could understand, as the strange craft drifted toward our side.

As the craft came closer, ropes were thrown on deck. To us watching it, it seemed a long time before the Flying Dutchman (such was its appearance) made fast. Then a boarding ladder was dropped down.

The two seamen, Vasconzelos and Kutschfreund, clambered down to ward off and protect the *Sierra Sagrada* from being smashed against the *Hornsee*'s side.

The mariner, who introduced himself as Frank Brenton, climbed on board. Thin and haggard, bearded and bedecked with a crust of salt, clothed in a field jacket and coat, he stood in stocking feet before the captain and thanked him for stopping.

Captain Schroder was not very enthusiastic, and probably felt none too friendly at first. But there was something else. We wondered if we were doing this for a genuinely shipwrecked mariner or a solo-sailing suicide candidate.

To the captain's question, "What the hell are you doing in this wide-open ocean with this goddamned junky outfit? Are you crazy?" the mariner nodded affirmatively.

He then answered that he wanted nothing more than water. [This is in error. The water was most welcome, but the first thing I wanted—and got—was my navigational position.]

We could not stand around on deck. It was neither practical nor hospitable, and the captain took him to the main saloon. We now knew him to be English-born, from America. This was an excellent chance for a hybrid question: "What will you have, coffee or tea?" Would his English birth or his American background show?

He disappointed us all by asking for lemonade. He could not drink fast enough. So fast did Brenton carry the glass to his mouth that Tank the bartender [what an appropriate name] could not keep pace with him. Just one moment and the glass was empty.

The remainder of the flask was swiftly poured, but even quicker went the emptying. Just as fast, the second bottle of *Frisco* lemonade was poured and drunk. Within seven minutes seven bottles of *Frisco* were drunk [I think you exaggerate here, Alex]. Sandwiches were set before him, but these were not viewed with anywhere near the same urgency. The main thing that seemed to plague him was thirst. Slowly his eyes brightened, and he began to talk.

It seems he thought he was south of the Azores. He knew he was in the Atlantic but was not sure where. When he found he was hundreds of miles northeast of Flores, he showed complete unconcern. In his opinion he was so close to Africa that he could almost touch it.

"Only a cuppla weeks," he said optimistically.

The cook in the meantime had readied a box of provisions and fruit. Tank the barkeeper offered a case of beer. And the deck-seamen had a water hose prepared to replenish his water supply. Frank said he would rather stow these things himself, so he climbed aboard the *Sierra Sagrada* again. As he shone his flashlight about, one could regard his boat a little closer.

Between the two decks was fastened an outboard motor on an iron bracket. The necessary gasoline stood in cans on the outrigger deck. The motor apparently was to be used to stay off unfriendly coasts and to furnish the accompanying music when he wanted to run into harbor.

Frank stowed the provisions in the innards of his boat and then came on deck and grabbed a waterline we trailed to him. He used an empty gasoline can, which seemed to serve for water also.

Hardly had he inserted the water hose than a rusty yellow flood gushed forth from the opening. If anyone believed he would rinse the can first, he was fooling himself. The crew yelled down hints to him, but, "Water is water," is all Frank yelled back.

On the biggest of his canoes were more cans, carefully lashed and covered with plastic and tarpaulin. He said that these contained calcium nitrate [this should be calcium hydride] and that the covers were to prevent the forcible entrance of water. His "pet" is what he called it.

After Frank had stowed his belongings, he clambered aboard the *Hornsee* once more, and he gave autographed copies of a book he had written to Captain Schroder and Chief Mate Schuldt.

As we talked in more general terms, we learned that because of a storm his transistor radio was sea-soaked and ruined. To the question of how he found his position, he said he had his "chronometer," which turned out to be an ordinary pocket watch that looked as though it came out of his grandfather's times. This happened to be three hours off [it had stopped], so he reset it. He could not set lights at night, for besides one pocket lamp [flashlight] he had no emergency lights. His only collision protection was a small radar reflector, bent into an *S* shape and nailed to the masthead.

Upon the question of what would happen if a ship ran over him in the darkness and vastness of the night, he pondered a brief moment and said, "They'll just lose a little paint."

Frank took his leave, after receiving his position, one of our ship's charts and our best regards. One could perceive that it was not easy. Perhaps he fought with himself to stay on board. Had he tasted too much civilization?

But true to his conviction, he swung on board the *Sierra Sagrada* and Vasconzelos and Kutschfreund returned to the deck. They were very relieved to have a single, massive, solid floor under their feet once more.

The mooring ropes were released, and slowly and carefully the *Sierra Sagrada* moved out and past our stern. Frank was left to his own abandon. Three long blasts gave him our farewell, and in the glare of our spotlight we could see him waving.

Long into the night we talked over the event, and there were not many who gave him a chance of survival. Over the value of such a trip our opinions were divided. Nevertheless, for us it was a diversion in the monotony of repetitious days at sea, and all of us wished him luck.

# Chapter X

I DID not know about Alex's version of what had happened at the time. I was too busy basking in the warm comfort of the *Hornsee*'s hospitality.

Captain Schroder was the same age as myself. He had once skippered a fishing craft for five years in the Baltic and further north.

"Sometimes I do not know if we had more water inside or out," he said.

He knew exactly how I felt.

The *Hornsee* was a tidy ship. Captain Schroder evidently took a lot of pride in his responsibilities and position, and it was just as much a delight to listen as it was to talk.

The *Hornsee* plied cargo between the Caribbean and Germany. On this voyage it was en route to France with a widely varied cargo, including fishmeal, zinc concentrate, coffee and cotton, from Peru, Colombia and Chile. There were also 12 passengers aboard, the maximum number allowed to be carried without carrying a regular ship's doctor.

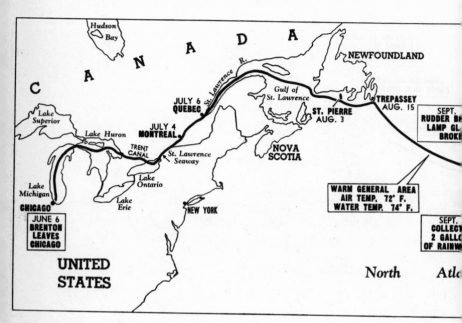

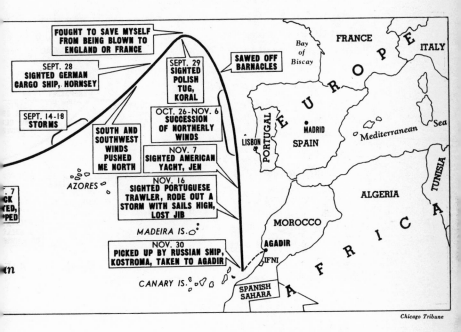

FOUGHT TO SAVE MYSELF FROM BEING BLOWN TO ENGLAND OR FRANCE

SEPT. 28 SIGHTED GERMAN CARGO SHIP, HORNSEY

SEPT. 29 SIGHTED POLISH TUG, KORAL

SAWED OFF BARNACLES

SEPT. 14-18 STORMS

OCT. 26-NOV. 6 SUCCESSION OF NORTHERLY WINDS

SOUTH AND SOUTHWEST WINDS PUSHED ME NORTH

NOV. 7 SIGHTED AMERICAN YACHT, JEN

AZORES

NOV. 16 SIGHTED PORTUGUESE TRAWLER, RODE OUT A STORM WITH SAILS HIGH, LOST JIB

MADEIRA IS.

NOV. 30 PICKED UP BY RUSSIAN SHIP, KOSTROMA, TAKEN TO AGADIR

CANARY IS.

SPANISH SAHARA

AGADIR

IFNI

MOROCCO

ALGERIA

TUNISIA

AFRICA

EUROPE

FRANCE

ITALY

Bay of Biscay

PORTUGAL

SPAIN

MADRID

LISBON

Mediterranean

Sea

*Chicago Tribune*

Captain Schroder spoke English and also Spanish, and the few other officers present also spoke English.

Hospitality is one thing, but I could not stop a ship indefinitely just to be sociable. A ship costs a lot of money an hour to run. I couldn't go on munching sandwiches forever.

But that did not stop me from telling them of my journey, and of what I hoped to achieve. I must have been aboard a couple of hours. Or maybe it was only fifty minutes. I lost count of time completely. We left along the ship's corridor, which was lined with curious ship's crew and passengers.

"Good heavens, man. What has happened to your shoes!" one passenger ejaculated.

I had come aboard in a heavy raincoat and parka and in bare stocking feet.

"If it is good enough dress for the *Sierra Sagrada*, it is good enough for the *Hornsee*," I blustered. I knew where my shoes were stowed, but I had not been able to find them.

Captain Schroder had asked me what supplies I needed, and I had told him bread, a case of beer, some fruit and milk. These he had sent aboard, and I scrambled down to stow them.

In all too small return I had left Captain Schroder and Chief Mate Schuldt each an autographed copy of *Long Sail to Haiti*. My wallet and traveler's checks were also hidden some place in my hold, but I had no idea where, so I couldn't even offer to pay for the supplies.

The voyage so far had done me no harm except to give me a king-sized thirst and an urge to talk to someone other than myself. Maybe I should have tried to buy a radio aboard or a watch. But although these things had been such a terrible concern to me over the past month, when I was on board the *Hornsee*, I completely forgot every problem I had.

Lest there be criticism: How many people have walked around all day with a letter in their pocket that they should have mailed, or talked over the phone for half an hour, then forgetting why they phoned? I made the same error on the *Hornsee*.

Captain Schroder had noticed I had salt-sores on the back of my wrists, where the wet sleeves had chafed. A bottle of aureomycin capsules plus salve were put in my pocket to take care of this.

My fresh water problems were also over. A crew member let down a hose and I filled a six-gallon drum. This was more than sufficient for the rest of the trip. Sixty-two days later I had used little more than four of the gallons, although I had consumed a case of beer and also a case of canned milk.

Finally, before 1 left the *Hornsee* I had asked if they would send a cable to Lois Lundy, my ball-of-fire public relations girl at the Field Museum.

It was a tremendous relief to be provisioned anew and to know my position. That was nothing to the relief of Kutschfreund and Vasconzelos, the two matelots detailed to guard the *Sierra Sagrada*. They fairly flew up the ladder as they handed their command back to me.

I suppose that standing on the deck of a canoe in mid-ocean, having only a bare nine inches of freeboard and all the time being washed ten feet up and down an oceangoing ship in a healthy swell (for however long it must have been), must have been more than a little nerve-wracking.

As the lines were withdrawn, the *Sierra Sagrada* drifted along the *Hornsee*'s side, giving me one anxious minute when my masts slipped under the overhanging angle of the ship's stern, before passing into the open sea.

A voice from the ship's side called, "Are you all right?" And I yelled back, "Yes."

The *Hornsee* started her engines, gave three hoots on her klaxon and went on her way. It was 10:00 P.M. on an almost moonless night. A spotlight played on me from the *Hornsee*'s bridge for a while, before it finally faded out of range.

I felt kind of lonely as I watched the *Hornsee* grow ever smaller, until she was a small white dot on the horizon. Then that also vanished, and I was back in the empty sea once more. My cabin space was packed with supplies, and I was loath to put them away just yet. So I slipped a blanket over my knees and slept cradled by the stacked provisions for the night.

I awakened early next morning to check the bags and boxes. What sounds commonplace on shore is luxury at sea: 24 pint-bottles of *Holsten* beer; 48 15-ounce cans of *Gluckslee* evaporated milk; apples, oranges, bananas and lemons to last me a week; five kilos of rye breads—*Weibrodt* (a light wheat bread), two loaves of *Graubrot* (a gray bread of mixed rye and wheat) and one loaf of *Schwarzbrot* (a black rye bread, which would last just about indefinitely); and half a kilo of fresh Dutch butter. This may not be much by store standards, but I had a "munchothon" as I sailed that day.

In any case, it was now back to the routine of sailing. I hoped to aim directly for Madeira, which was some 600 miles almost due south. "No problem at all," I thought.

The morning also brought wind from the southwest, but I figured it was sure to change to north or west. All the sailing manuals and pilot charts said north or west winds prevailed; I would breeze into Madeira Island within 20 days at the maximum.

I was wrong. For the following 29 days the wind remained south or southwest. They were all fine sailing days, but unfortunately they were ideal only for sailing in the wrong direction. Twenty-nine days later I was in the Bay of Biscay, still 600 miles from Madeira.

I cussed like a trooper, but it did no good. It was literally a problem to prevent myself from being blown to England or France. That whole month I was probably the most reluctant Atlantic-crosser on the high seas. The big trouble was that if I did reach Europe I would not have sufficient funds to buy gasoline to motor down to Africa. So I stayed in the deep Atlantic, to make as much use of the winds as possible.

On October 29th, my 75th day, the north winds at last began to reassert themselves, and I stayed at the tiller 18 hours a day until I had passed Portugal and the European coast completely. But this takes a lot of time and a fair amount of events, so I will backtrack a little.

After I left the *Hornsee,* the weather set a new pattern: a cycle that took in approximately four or five days. Wind would come gently from a southwest direction the first day. Then it would increase in strength, until by the time it had reached some 25 to 30 knots a bank of clouds would have appeared as a weather front from the northwest. The southwest wind would then reach a burst of frenzy, with froth and spray howling along the sea-tops like mountainous balls of suds. Then a heavy wind would wash the southwest wind away completely, and a fair northwest wind would take its place. This northwest wind would never last more than a day before a languid calm would take its place. After the calm, the cycle would start once more.

October 9th brought one of those calms. No wind blew worthy of the name, and I had stripped down my motor to remove salt accumulations from the carburetor. The *Koral,* a Polish tugboat from Gnydia on its way to Trinidad, appeared on the horizon, making straight for my position.

It made a passing arc before motoring alongside to see if I needed assistance, and I got a new position of 42° 57′ north and 16° 09′ west. It had taken me 11 days to sail 140 miles south!

The crew offered me provisions, too, but I already was well stocked with the provisions from the *Hornsee*. Also, although the sea was calm by my usual standards, the *Koral* was rolling badly. Unlike the smooth flat surface of normal ships' sides, the *Koral*'s sides were armored all around with the heavy iron fenders of an ocean-going tug. The *Koral* went on its way. I reassembled the motor and cranked it to make sure it worked.

It would have been pleasant to have motored all day, but I did not have sufficient gasoline. All the way across on the voyage I had to be satisfied with starting the motor every two or three days, running it for five minutes and then shutting it down and covering it again.

The Johnson was a godsend. I nursed it like a newborn babe and covered it with lengths of discarded shirt and plastic, and it never gave me any trouble. The motor was used mostly to investigate stray floating cases or float-supported fishnet, all of which were in abundance in the sea, or any other drifting material which happened to float within reach. I never saw anything of value, except a 55-gallon drum of diesel fuel, which bounced heavily against my side before I let it go once more. Yet although I didn't find anything valuable, motoring over just to poke around and explore was fun and entertaining on its own account.

It was at the time I met the *Koral* that I noted I had a cold. "Absurd," I thought. "Colds cannot be caught at sea." But sure enough, I now had a runny nose. I must have caught it during my brief stay aboard the *Hornsee*. I had no way of knowing how much resistance I had or of knowing if the present cold could develop into a serious infection. As a precaution, I took three antibiotic tablets over an eight-hour period.

With the motor checked out and the *Koral* under way, I relaxed in the shelter of my cabin. With my feet in my sleeping bag and a blanket over my knees, I brought my diaries up to date and once more went over my projected courses if the weather chose to change.

Colds come in a rush, hang around for a while and then fade imperceptibly, as though forgotten. This was no exception; apart from a runny-nose rawness caused by the open air, the cold was gone in two or three days. As a bonus, the tablets had healed and dried the salt-sore chafing around my wrists, and I was back to my normal self. I took the list of provisions that I had received from the *Hornsee*, and under the last itemized entry I added, "Plus one cold."

One consolation was that the days were becoming noticeably warmer the further south I sailed. But instead of having less to do, more chores accumulated as the days passed—day-to-day chores, which could not be avoided. Sometimes I washed my outer clothes and hung them in the rigging to dry. Old salt was mostly replaced by new salt, and grease spots from the motor remained embedded. But it was not a complete waste of time, for it boosted my morale. In the Caribbean I had trailed the clothes behind me in the boat's churning wake, but just now speed was at a premium, and I needed every inch I could get, so I could afford no extra drag.

So many barnacles had accumulated under my hull that my original progress had been almost cut in half. From more than three knots at the start of the journey, I was now lucky to make two knots with a howling gale and full sail hoisted.

I had a veritable garden below me. Goosenecked barnacles three or four inches long grew so thick and close together that the bottom of the hull felt like sponge rubber. Copper-painting at Newfoundland would have helped, but I have learned from experience that nothing can fully prevent goosenecked barnacles from establishing themselves—and in any case, there had been no copper-painting, so the question was academic.

Keel-hauling a strop of wood along each of the hulls, in much the same manner as a shoeshiner strops a pair of shoes, had kept the barnacles under control for a while. But as individual barnacles became stronger, so the method became less efficient and finally of almost no value whatsoever.

In the Caribbean I had swum and had scraped the barnacles clean at the same time. But sharks were becoming frequent visitors, and also the Atlantic waters were far too cold.

Eventually I hit upon the idea of sawing the barnacles away; as most of the *Sierra Sagrada*'s surfaces are flat or convex, it seemed an ideal method. The deepest part of the lowest "V" of my pontoon was a bare 15 inches under water. My 24-inch woodsaw was more than adequate.

In this way I passed many hours of many days: one arm underwater sawing barnacle stems and hoping no hungry sharks or similar beasts cared to follow upward the long banner of succulent barnacles that trailed to the depths below. Only one small strip proved inaccessible, the part along my main canoe, which was too wide for me to reach under with the saw.

Even goosenecked barnacles have their own merits at

sea. There is no more diligent sweeper, for they cling to anything and everything. I have even seen whales and turtles with goosenecked barnacles plastered all over their hides. Discarded bottles and light bulbs and other flotsam are otherwise unsinkable until accumulating barnacles build to such a weight that they sink to the depths, and the ocean's pressure does the rest.

But for all their merits, I felt I could do without the barnacles, of which I estimated that I must have had 300 pounds under my hulls. Barnacles were 90 percent water, so their weight was not a tremendous factor, but their feeding *cirri*, probing before them, acted as thousands of small anchors.

Barnacles also are a part of the daily diet in many parts of the world. In Arab lands they are a delicacy. Their taste is similar to mussels or oysters, and for any stranded mariner who tends toward shellfish foods living off barnacles alone would present no problem. It is unfortunate that I am not keen on mussels or oysters, nor am I keen on barnacles. However, I know they are edible, for I ate them as a regular diet before the journey was over. But that story comes later.

A white shark put in an appearance shortly after one of my early morning barnacle-cleaning days. He was quite lean and about eight feet long. Frequently at night sharks would scrape along my hull. The sound was unmistakable. Usually they finished by running into my rudder, which clanged up and down as though hit by a hammer.

This fellow did the same. It was a tragic error, for I happened to be cleaning my .22 Savage at the time. The shark hit the rudder, then turned for another run, smooching alongside my cabin near the strap at the fore of the cabin. He presented me with a fine grin of white pointed teeth and an unprotected gullet: I cocked the rifle and shot him in the underside of his head. His eyes were already glazed as he took a shallow 30-degree glide into the depths, his broad shovel-like tail working by reflex only. He was already as dead a shark as I have ever seen.

I do not like sharks.

I was astounded at the amount of sealife in the colder regions of the North Atlantic—not the great quantities of flying fish I was accustomed to in warmer waters, but a constant procession of whales and sharks, along with a never-ending procession of fish the size of cod and pilchard. Small rays played on the surface of the water, and I saw my first *manta*, a giant of a fellow, fully eight feet across, which leaped across the water like a delta-winged jet. I consoled myself by deciding that this was a legitimate reason for my lack of success while fishing. They had better bait than I could offer.

Birdlife was so common at the 45th parallel when I met the *Hornsee* that I took it for granted I was coasting near the Azores. There were fully a dozen different species, but at yet, I have no idea what they were.

From the 45th parallel to the 30th parallel, the latitude of the Canary Islands, is a distance of about 1,000 miles, and my sails and rigging took the brunt of the constant buffeting as I battled headwinds and crosswinds. Hardly a day passed without one repair or another being needed.

I found myself saving food or beer as compensation for these small tasks. Sewing the fraying edge of the mainsail was worth an extra spoonful of sugar (or marmalade, if I fancied) with diluted evaporated milk. A session of bar-nacle-cutting merited a beer. A headwind or a calm, when I left my sails furled, meant either no food at all or a drastic reduction. For each hour at the tiller past sundown, I collected an extra hard candy while they lasted. The principle applied was that of a case of taskmaster and worker.

This experience of a dual personality when at sea by oneself has been noted so often that it must be real. Joshua Slocum had a helmsman at his tiller when he had eaten too much cheese and plums on his journey from Horta to Gibraltar. Francis Chichester swore that someone was aboard on his return from Australia. I never quite reached that stage, but when a loose rope tapped me on the shoulder while I was absorbed in the sea, I turned around to see who it was rather than what it was. Talking to oneself is by no means unhealthy, yet after some 80 days I started getting unexpected replies.

A splash appeared on the horizon. "That's a giant breaker," I said aloud, returning my attention to the tiller.

"That's not a breaking wave. It's a whale," something distinctly answered.

"By Jove, you are right," I said—and then I felt somehow ridiculous about the whole thing.

Boredom is never present. "Always something to do" is the theme of all genuine sailors. Maybe people easily bored do not look far for things to do; I do not have the qualifications to guess. Nevertheless, during the whole 106 days at sea, I seemed to be busy all the time.

On my 84th day I met the *Jen*, a deep-sea cruising-yacht hailing from New York. At the time, she was on her way to the Canary Islands from Lisbon. I saw her on the horizon and as she was traveling a parallel course, started my motor and took off after her.

The day was calm, with no more than a two- or three-knot wind. She saw that I was following behind and dropped back to see if I needed help.

Mainly, I wanted to know Greenwich mean time. A

number of good sun-readings, combined with my pocket watch's not having stopped for three days, had told me I was near the 35th parallel. Greenwich mean time would give me longitude.

The answer to my query was expedited by the crew's having electronic position-finding equipment aboard, and they gave my position as 35° 32′ north and 12° 20′ west. Now I knew what direction to aim and how far I was from the African coast in the event of emergencies.

I had hoped to buy extra food and had $20 in small bills in front of me, but they were also short on provisions. As they would be in the Canary Islands so much sooner than I, they did donate two two-pound cans of peaches, one two-pound can of ravioli, one two-pound can of sausage and beans and some biscuits and fruit. In exchange, and as an enterprising writer, I left them with an autographed copy of *Long Sail to Haiti*.

The position given me by the *Jen* told me that I had some 350 miles to go to Lanzarote, the closest of the Canary Islands. Once again, therefore, I turned to my pilot-chart to calculate the wind probabilities and found out that northerly winds had a 64 percent chance of blowing in November. Consequently, I little doubted that I would soon be in a safe harbor.

I kept lazing along, sometimes with a ship on the horizon, often with only clouds or an occasional swell. My faith in the *Sierra Sagrada* was such that not for one moment would I consider she might let me down. With this confidence I could conserve all my energy for sailing.

I came to recognize every peculiarity of the craft. Little things that did not appear important at the time grated if they seemed out of place. Once I remember the jib looked somehow askew, as though not bellied in quite the right shape. I went forward to check and found that the running rigging had caught in a frayed wire on the jib-stay. If it had been left like that for a few hours, it would have worn the nylon-line, and I would have had to shin up the mast with a new replacement.

It was little things like this that kept the *Sierra Sagrada* shipshape. Maybe I could not go below the hull and clean barnacles as perfectly as I would have liked, but topsides were always in near perfect condition. At least, then, it can be said that even when I was lazing away the time, my mind was as busy as ever.

But even lazing about wears thin as an occupation, and a faint voice was beginning to ask, "Will this journey never end?"

Over the horizon was Africa, and I knew I would soon be there. Patience was all I needed—patience, that is, and a favorable wind.

# Chapter XI

Once past Europe I started taking my position far more seriously. Below the trade-wind zone I had taken it for granted that weather was likely to be inconsistent, but south of the Mediterranean zone I certainly had sound reason to expect better weather than I received.

Again, it was steady plodding. "Two days forward and one day back," I noted in my log. My pilot-charts said that there was an 82 percent chance of winds in my favor, against only a 15 percent chance of winds from the contrary south and 3 percent chance of calms. However, south winds still blew as hard as ever, regardless of what the pilot-chart said. By my 99th day I estimated that I was still about 12 degrees west and 200 miles south of Lanzarote.

My food supply was fast becoming desperate. All that remained were one two-pound can of peaches, one nineteen-ounce can of beans and two cans of evaporated milk. However, I still had more than two gallons of water left, so water was no problem.

A few days earlier I had thrown away my last can of

The *Sierra Sagrada* in
the Field Museum of
Natural History.

Three canoes breaking the ice on the Chicago River on New Year's Day.

Leaving Chicago's Diversey Harbor.

Humidity meter, barometer, and thermometer on cabin top; second thermometer on mast.

Fending off the *Sierra Sagrada* from the *Hornsee*.

"Ah, fill that up!" Aboard the *Hornsee*.

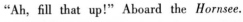

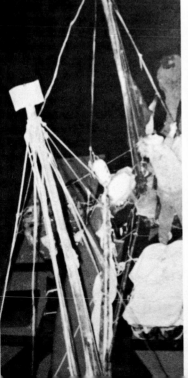

Checking deck fittings and motor while becalmed.

Jottings in the *Sierra Sagrada's* weather log.

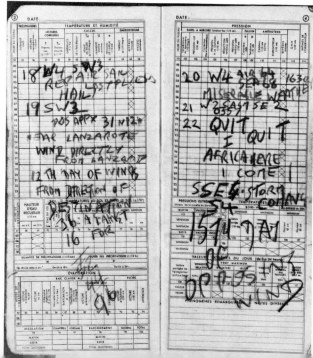

On the deck of the *Kostroma*.

Rudder being checked aboard the
*Kostroma*.

Self-portrait at sea.

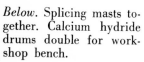

*Above*. Rust accumulation from 106-day journey—no shortage of iron rations!

*Right*. Henri and Arlette Bassinet and their child.

*Below*. Splicing masts together. Calcium hydride drums double for workshop bench.

*Above*. Rural scene in Gambia.

*Left*. Peanut farmers using *fantingo* hoes in Gambia.

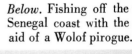

*Below*. Fishing off the Senegal coast with the aid of a Wolof pirogue.

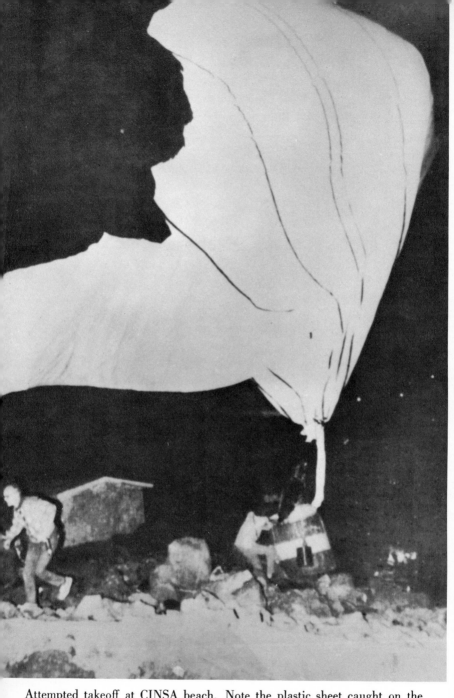

Attempted takeoff at CINSA beach. Note the plastic sheet caught on the top of the balloon.

sardines, for they had shown a suspicious bulge, and botulism is always a danger in any canned meats. A can of baked beans had also blown, but these were vegetarian beans without pork and therefore unlikely to be seriously affected. Indeed, when I tasted them I was surprised to find the flavor had slightly improved over the usual bland Campbell's flavor. They certainly did not need added condiments, for the spoiling had converted the sugar to acid, adding a *piquant* tang almost like a New World-Chinese brand of Boston baked beans.

I was mixing the evaporated milk to the formula half-milk and half-water and was allowing it to curdle to a yogurt. The curdling probably added further vitamins, and each can was rations for two days. Between meals I had been eating barnacles for the past few weeks. I ate them in Arab fashion: pull the barnacle, bite the end, and the meat inside the stem comes free.

From the survival point of view, a better fare was the green eelgrass growing on the waterline. I couldn't get enough of this, for it had a pleasant taste. It looked like spinach, and when it was squeezed dry between finger and thumb, it tasted like salted spinach, and it was no doubt jammed with vitamins.

"This was supposed to be one of the projects of the journey," I told myself. As I have said, one of my projects before starting on the journey had been to make notes of any survival ideas that might occur, but I never guessed that I would need to take the matter so seriously.

Even the mushrooms, which I had once despised, had long since been proved to be nonpoisonous. At first I had just nibbled on them. Then I had found that they were firm and sweet and quite up to commercial standards. If I had known a way to cultivate them, I certainly would have tried. As it was, I soon ate the hulls bare, for I doubt if there was a quarter of a cupful on the whole journey.

To return to more conventional sources of food, however: "Ten days to go," I thought, as I checked my minuscule supply of normal canned food. The can of peaches could last me three days, the beans a further three days and the cans of milk two days each. "Fourteen days, if I stretch it a little," I calculated.

Food now was to be largely what I could collect from the sea. It was a fisherman's life, and one on which I could survive almost indefinitely, or at least until I could get back to more wholesome meals again.

My world narrowed to food and weather. The food I could cope with, but the weather was as big a problem as ever. Another calm set in, and I was on pins and needles waiting to see which way the wind would spring. Small breezes flickered from every direction. At three o'clock in the afternoon a faint wind blew from the north, and I was jubilant. Then it died away, leaving the sea with a troubled, ominous-looking sheen.

Slowly the breeze mounted from south-southeast, and the sheen became rippled jags. The wind mounted and had that hollow howl as though it was here to stay. I expected a southern storm that night, and I battened down and furled the mainsail, leaving jib and mizzen close-hauled to save the precious miles I would lose if I remained baremasted. I even entered in the log that a storm was on its way.

But I was wrong. The wind that night stayed steady and the following day was sunny. Everything was right except that the wind was blowing from exactly the wrong direction. It was blowing from due south, over the bows.

"I QUIT," I wrote in my log.

Again I was wrong. One cannot quit while at sea. All one can do is to continue to try. And if that does not work, then try a little bit harder.

"Maybe I could sail to Agadir or Mogador, on the Moroccan coast," I thought. This was a desperate idea, for both were behind me, and both were a further distance than the Canary Islands.

An even stronger objection was that in doing so I could be beset by a westerly gale while exposed on the open coast. Islands I could motor around until I reached their lee; on an open coast I would need to anchor on an extreme anchor line and wait for favorable winds, or I would have to risk sailing in search of a coastal harbor.

I decided that an open coast could easily be a suicide-trap and made a weather-log of the winds since leaving the *Hornsee.* Despite the percentages indicated on the pilot-chart, the log showed that calms occurred almost without fail no more than seven days apart. After every calm a southerly wind blew. The only exception to this was from October 26th to November 3rd, when I enjoyed eight uninterrupted days of northerly winds, which took me all the way down the Portuguese coast and almost to my present position.

What dastardly weather it had been! Yet even though I could expect this southerly weather to continue at least for a few more days, I was scrambling forward at approximately 18 miles a day. Partly the reason was that I was still on the southerly-flowing section to the gulf stream, which provided a theoretical 12-mile-a-day current in my favor. However, I suspected that the surface waters had long ago been brought to a halt by the continual adverse winds, and that this current, as far as I was concerned, was now virtually non-existent.

At lower depths, of course, the flow would still be as

strong as ever, I realized. And if I had had a very large sea-anchor, I could have lowered this into the depths and used the deeper current to drag me along.

German U-boats used this system frequently during the war. When they wished to leave the Mediterranean, they sank to the lower depths, cut their motor and drifted out with the heavier salt water that spilled over the Gibraltar Strait shelf into the deeper Atlantic—not that this useless piece of information would do me any good.

With 120 more miles to go, I had a fair chance of reaching shore within six or seven days, and I prepared for a siege. I built a plankton-net of a cotton shirt, braced with the remainder of the close-weave, wire-gauze netting I had used to protect my Coleman lamp from salt water and splashes. Plankton was now added to my fare of barnacles and eelgrass. If I kept on like this, I would soon be blowing like a whale.

I had studied survival at sea in an academic way and had knowingly spoken of being able to live off plankton, for even the most amateur oceanographer has written reams about the nutritional delights of the lowly plankton. Now it seemed as though I would have to eat my very words.

What I had not realized—and what no one seems to have stressed—is that one needs a net fully a yard across and that this net gets frayed and torn. My net acted as a sea-anchor at the wrong level. Without doubt, plankton is an excellent survival food, but it is certainly overrated.

The look of plankton is more distasteful than its flavor. Plankton is only a minute form of sealife, and this was no time to dwell on looks and fancy preparations or so I rationalized. Surely small crustaceans cannot be any worse than such large crustaceans as shrimp, crab or lobster. Small fish or eggs are no worse than large fish or caviar. Minute jellyfish do not fit into any regular pattern, unless they can be compared to octopus or squid, which are delicacies of many people's choice. Plankton, then, is just a large meal on a small scale.

There are poisonous plankton organisms, but fortunately these are rare. Instead of thinking of my meal as barnacles, eelgrass, jellyfish eggs and plankton, I thought of it as oysters, spinach, squid and shrimp. I trusted my stomach to be too famished to notice the difference, and I found that these foods did slide down very easily.

The southerly wind blew ever stronger, and it brought a guest on board: an exhausted fluff of a canary. This was proof of how close I was to land, and I knew that perseverance would bring results.

The canary cheeped and fretted from rigging to rigging, searching in vain for a sheltered spot. It first tried to hide between the chemical drums, but occasional waves would buffet through, and the canary emerged wetter than ever. Then it tried sheltering behind the mainsail, but it could not grasp a foothold. Finally it settled in the upper fork of my mizzen gaff.

I looked at him hungrily, wondering whether to have canary for dinner. With gun and net and such a dismal, tired bird, I could hardly miss. However, I also happen to like the company of wild life. Dismissing him as too small to make a decent mouthful, I let him be. The elementary law of the sea demands that one does not abuse a companion in distress.

As the afternoon wore on, the wind strengthened, and gusts suggested it would be a tempestuous night. The canary cheeped and fretted more than ever, as he clung tight for dear life. About an hour before sundown he left his perch and scooted eastward, flying low between the waves of the

now turbulent sea. His direction of departure was signifi-
cant to me: I had to be close to the African coast. But it also
saddened me. With those winds and the probable distance
to shore, my poor little friend probably never had a chance.
Land was still nowhere in sight.

The storm continued for two full days and a night.
"Force 10," I put down in my log. To have left the sails
unfurled would have meant being blown back by the
violent winds, and I stayed awake most of the night stretching the canvas and trying vainly to make headway without
tearing the overburdened sheets.

Daytime was not too bad. Breaking waves could be
judged with accuracy. Night was black, for the moon had
waned to a mere disk. However, while my sails were aloft,
I still made progress, and I rode with mizzen and mainsail
high.

The wind slowly died away, until by mid-afternoon
the sea was calm. I brought out my needle and line and spent
the next few hours sewing the weakened sail-seams. By
nightfall the sea was as smooth as glass, so I resigned myself
for another calm and turned in for the night.

It must have been about 3:00 A.M. when I was awakened
by the high-pitched whine of wind and the slap of wavelets
against my hull as they built up force. "Not again," I
thought in desperation. Yet I knew that another gale was
on its way.

I opened my hatch cover and looked up at a smattering
of stars. My wind sock bellowed healthily in the wind; the
star pattern was the other way around. A north wind at
last! *I could not believe it!*

I flashed my light over the face of the compass to make
sure. Yes, the wind was certainly from the north: I just

hoped the trade winds had resumed their normal course.

It had been 21 days since I last sailed under a north wind, and I wasted no time. I put the port jib up and then the mainsail. The starboard jib and mizzen were already drawing, and I started picking up speed.

The wind was now Force 5, the equivalent of a blustery day by land standards. This must have been the reason for the previous night of storm. The weather pattern had not yet completely broken, but the trade winds were slowly taking control.

I stayed at the tiller 26 hours that stretch, squeezing every mile I could out of the wind. Food was forgotten for the first time in weeks. All I was concerned about was making progress and reaching land. About 5:00 A.M. the next morning I reluctantly set the *Sierra Sagrada* to sail on her own while I snatched forty winks of sleep before sunrise.

I would have preferred to have stayed at the tiller and to have set a direct southerly course, but my jibs had taken the worst beating of the sea voyage, and they were barely half their original size. Southeast was the nearest course I could secure.

Water splashes had soaked my clothes long ago, and my cabin was far from dry. I did not even notice the discomfort. I pulled my blanket over my knees and dropped into a sleep of complete exhaustion.

Habits are not easy to break, and I awoke at sunrise, as I had known I would. The wind was as strong as ever, and I opened the last can of beans for breakfast. I had eaten the peaches the previous day, and all I had left were the two cans of evaporated milk plus a whole boatload of barnacles. I chose not to think of the food situation and took my position at the tiller once more.

A new series of ships appeared in a strange north-south

direction. I checked my chart but could make little sense of their course. Then I shrugged it off, thinking I had misjudged their direction.

In fact, I was nearing the west coast of Africa; not having a reliable way of knowing the time, I had misjudged my longitude. While I was still searching for Lanzarote, I had actually passed east of the island and was now in the Cape Juby passage.

That night I stayed at the tiller until past midnight. Then the wind slackened until it did not warrant the effort to stay awake any longer. It was time I caught up with the sleep I had lost the previous night.

November 30th, my 106th day at sea, was calm with light airs from the west. I set the tiller and spent the day drying clothes and making minor repairs to my rigging and motor. Late in the afternoon a ship appeared on the horizon, heading directly in my direction. A desperate position called for desperate measures. My sails were still aloft, so I dropped them. Then I got my navigation board and waved it, and waved it, and waved it. If I knew my position, I would know where to aim. Maybe I could even motor there if the distance was less than 50 miles.

As the ship came closer, I could see that it was the tanker *Kostroma,* a Russian ship. I have never known a Russian ship yet that could resist the temptation of coming over to find out what was going on, and I was confident she would stop.

The backward churning of the ship's propellers told me that the *Kostroma* was slackening speed. She made a slow half-turn. No prejudice is implied here, but she did not have the seamanship of the German *Hornsee.*

"That is strange," I thought. "She is coming in on my lee, and I am going to bounce heavily against her side."

That was my last opportunity for thought, because I was immediately too busy warding-off to ask any questions. A line was dropped over the side, and I tied it to a deck fastening. Then a rope ladder was dropped down to my deck, and a Russian crew member scrambled aboard.

"Good. He can ward-off while I find where I am," I beamed. "Do you know my position?" I yelled up to the bridge.

"Da," someone shouted back.

That did not seem to be a very good start, so I tried again. "I have lost my radio and clock and do not know my position," I yelled.

"Da," half a dozen of the crew shouted back.

Looking over my shoulder I saw that my "assistant" had hauled a two-inch-diameter rope aboard and was giving it a final knot as he tied it around my mizzen mast.

"Hold it!" I yelled, and diving over the gas tanks and kayak, I wrestled the knot undone and threw the rope overboard.

I was nowhere near fast enough. My rescuer already had a second two-inch rope secured to my foremast and was beckoning a winch-member to make it tight.

"Cut that out!" I screamed.

"Da," said my helper, and I watched in horror as the rope got tighter and the mast bent forward.

*Crash!* As the mast snapped in two, the whole rigging collapsed in a junk-heap of wire.

I felt sick to my stomach. "You've really fouled things up," I said.

"Da," said my helper dismally.

By now it had dawned on me what had happened. The Russian ship had seen me waving frantically, and the *Sierra Sagrada* was so low in the water that they thought I was sinking. Therefore, I had been *rescued*, and I was going to be put on the *Kostroma*'s deck. The only trouble was that I had not wanted to be rescued.

I scrambled up the ship's ladder and over the rails. A chubby, sad-faced man helped me. "I am Captain Agibalov," he introduced himself in halting English, as we ceremoniously shook hands. He wore no uniform, and he had the air of a beardless, chastised Santa Claus whose good intentions had somehow gone wrong.

"I did not want to be rescued," I told him.

"What did you want?" he asked.

"I wanted to know my position," I said.

He thought it over.

"You are on the *Kostroma*," he said.

So, after 106 days, I at last knew without doubt where I was.

Life is a series of adjustments. It was now past sundown, and I had not changed my clothes for far too long to be sociable. The first things I craved were a shower, a shave, a haircut and a meal—in that order.

There was a shower fitting in the ship's hospital, but it did not work, so I substituted a bath instead. Then I borrowed a razor and soon emerged looking relatively civilized.

My hair hung over my ears like an out-of-work Tchaikovsky, and I had lost a lot of weight. Otherwise I was in good shape. The boatswain was much the same build as myself, and he loaned me a crisp set of clothes. Another crew member took my old gear away, and I received them back next day scrubbed and clean. What I really needed was a good meal.

The bath had given me an invigorating appetite, and I made my way along the companionways until I reached the amidships' saloon. Three officers were there just finishing a meal, and I mentioned that I was hungry, too. Never have I met such speedy, cooperative people. They fairly raced down to the galley and then put me at a table full of things I had been craving for weeks: hunks of cheese; tangy Polish sausage; thick, spongy, black bread; pickles and anchovies. I satisfied my initial hunger with a couple of slices of sausage and cheese and then made a super multi-layered sandwich from the other plates, washing everything down with hot tea poured from a silvered teapot.

The officers came back aghast. Dr. Nickolai Kuznezovsky explained that they had gone to order beef broth, a long-standing rehabilitation diet for shipwrecked and starving sailors. I was delighted.

"Excellent. I'll have it after I've had a couple more sandwiches," I told him.

Ah, what a pleasure it was to eat and to know I would not have to bounce on the ocean waves again that night. I was well over my initial disappointment of not having landed under my own power. The *Sierra Sagrada* had been safely lifted on deck, and stowed on blocks. Tomorrow I would look after it.

Our language barrier never appeared. We were all sailors, and with maps, gestures and a few mutual words we soon got to tell our tales. As I ate, I told them of the events that had led to my stopping the *Kostroma*.

In turn, they told me that the *Kostroma* had made a journey for oil to the Persian Gulf and that it was now on its way to Italy before proceeding to its final destination: Odessa, on the Black Sea. I also found out that Kostroma, the ship's namesake, is a city in midwest Russia, high on the Volga. The reason for such a roundabout route was that the Suez Canal was closed because of the recent Arab-Israeli war.

Captain Agibalov had by now joined us. "I was on my way to the Canary Islands," I told him. Then he showed me on a Russian chart that my position had been 29° north, 12° 30′ west. How ironical. One more day and I would have sighted land without fail.

"We can take you to Gibraltar," Captain Agibalov offered.

That was certainly too far north. It would mean an extra 600 miles of sailing and motoring merely to return to my present position. However, with a broken mast I could not be put over the side again. There are few ports along this section of the African coast, and a rapid calculation narrowed the choice to one.

"Can you take me to Agadir?" I asked.

Agadir was not far off the *Kostroma*'s route, and if the captain headed there he would arrive the following day in daylight hours.

It was plain that Captain Agibalov would have preferred to go to Gibraltar. He hesitated.

"Gibraltar is better?" he asked brightly.

"Agadir is closer," I countered.

Damn it, I should have been mad at him for half-wrecking my boat.

"We will see," he said sadly.

I had never been on a Russian ship before, and I wandered around at will. Dr. Kuznezovsky accompanied me. He spoke Russian and German; I spoke English and Spanish. We did not communicate.

By about nine o'clock in the evening, most of the crew had turned in for the night. Somewhere aft a balalaika was strumming, but apart from that the ship was asleep. After a brief tour of the bridge, I turned in also. A large tray of untouched bread and cheese was in the saloon, and I took this along to the ship's hospital, which was my cabin for the night.

The next morning dawned clear, and I checked the *Sierra Sagrada*. Apart from the broken mast, she appeared to have suffered no harm from the previous day's rough treatment. Patches of barnacles showed my remote-cleaning job not to have been wholly successful. The outboard motor was in the workshop, and sluggishness as I pulled the starting rope suggested that water was in the cylinders. The rudder had received a heavy blow against the ship's side, and a carpenter was repairing the fractured tip.

After a meal of boiled eggs and cheese, I helped Captain Agibalov prepare a statement for his superiors, and at the same time he told me that our expected time of arrival at Agadir was 3:00 P.M.

This had been the first trip away from Russian waters for most of the crew, and since it was the first time they had crossed the equator, they had been through the international ceremony of being ordained by King Neptune. Someone had the brilliant idea that he wanted my signature beside that of the illustrious monarch, and he brought his *Equator Diploma* for me to sign. I might have lost my beard, but my hair was long enough. I signed a flourishing:

> Welcome from King Neptune
> *Sierra Sagrada*
> Francis Brenton

It was an immediate success, and I spent half the morning signing everyone else's diplomas. Even shy Dya, the mess stewardess who nearly poured half the soup over me, brought hers to sign.

Dya, dear Dya. Surely your Russian friends were pulling

my leg. My Russian-English dictionary tells me that *Dya* means *uncle*. And you certainly were not uncle-ish.

The *Sierra Sagrada*'s rigging was still a knotted tangle of spars and wire, and the boatswain helped me untangle the mess. I cut the sails free from their fittings, and we un-raveled and uncoiled all the ropes and halyards. I would not be doing any sailing for a while, so I was really preparing the craft for dry-docking and overhauling.

Many of my clothes and my bedding were still wet, and I spread these over the deck to dry. The fourth engineer was also the barber, and I took thirty minutes from my tasks while he cut my hair. At last I felt civilized again.

After a leisurely midday meal the African coast ap-peared, so I restored my belongings to my cabin and lashed the spars firmly to the *Sierra Sagrada*'s deck.

Agadir presented itself as a white, tidy town, set on a plain with rolling hills around. The Casbah's fortress walls high on a mountain top strategically dominated the boat-laden artificial harbor and highway. Agadir is a rich district of Morocco. Its especially delicious sweet oranges, tanger-ines and tomatoes are exported to all parts of the world; small, sweet tangerines grown there are called clementines.

A tugboat left Agadir Harbor to meet us. Joe Manivet and Hubert Alleon came aboard and made arrangements to tow the *Sierra Sagrada* ashore. There would be no port duties for the *Kostroma* to pay.

The mastless *Sierra Sagrada* was slipped over the side, and I went up to the captain's cabin to say good-bye to Cap-tain Agibalov. Under a giant, grinning portrait of Lenin we shook hands. I certainly had no reason to be critical of the treatment I had received during my stay aboard the *Kostroma*.

In return, I had cooperated as much as possible and

presented a signed copy of *Long Sail to Haiti* to Captain Agibalov as a souvenir from a reluctant, but far from disgruntled, passenger. Captain Agibalov must have been looking at his phrase book for the proper thing to say.

"Thank you for a most unusual happening," he said.

*"Spasibo,"* I said in return.

I clambered down to my deck, threw the lines clear and made fast a heaving-line from the tug. The *Kostroma* gave three hoots, and her propellers slowly turned. I sat at the tiller behind the tug and helped guide my way to port. It had been quite a hectic crossing!

# Chapter XII

THERE were the usual routine formalities to attend to: immigration officials to see for permission to stay in Morocco; customs officials to declare the value of my craft; health authorities to show my papers. My first few hours ashore were a hustle of activity, and I was given permission to stay 30 days—more than sufficient time to make my craft seaworthy.

Cooperation by everyone was unstinted. Agadir Yacht Club offered full facilities of its workshops and of anything I required in tools or workmen.

Joe Manivet helped me with language problems. He could speak Moroccan, Spanish, French and English with equal ease. "Sometimes I forget which nationality I am," he said. He was supervisor and expeditor for Somatime, the Societe Maritime de Morocco. My French is poor at the best of times, and Joe was soon answering most of the questions about my voyage.

There were many other things to be done, and the first was to send Lois Lundy a brief cable: *106 days. Bent but safe. Newsletter follows. Fascinating journey. Frank.* When the newsletter would follow I did not know, for none of my notes were in order.

I also had to prepare the *Sierra Sagrada* for sea, and this promised to be an arduous task. The winds had been so treacherous for the past 60 days that I had made up my mind to head down the African coast as far as Dakar in search of a take-off site for my proposed aerial crossing of the Atlantic. I had already ascertained that my balloon plastic was still in perfect condition, and shaking the five-gallon drums proved that the calcium hydride also was dry. Low Altitude Flying Feat, Operation LAFF, was the next big project.

An odd and irritating thing had happened aboard the *Sierra Sagrada*. I could not find the $280 in traveler's checks that I had bought before leaving Newfoundland. Where they had gone I could not discover. They were of no value to anyone except myself, and they could easily be replaced. However, this would mean a delay while I got in touch with the bank at St. John's where they had been issued.

I remembered I had wrapped them in a tight plastic bag shortly before heading out to sea, but I went through every packet and searched along every shelf without bringing them to light, and I was forced to assume I had thrown them overboard during one of the more hectic bailing-out periods.

The final spree of selling my books in Trepassey had left me with more than $100 in Canadian and United States currency, so there was no real financial urgency. I resolved to send a letter at my earliest opportunity and temporarily shelved the problem.

The Cadarses invited me to dinner that evening. Robert Cadars was director of the port of Agadir, and I was honored and delighted to accept. Robert Cadars had been with the Free French forces in Britain during the war and, while staying in London, had married Jacquie, an English girl. They had remained in England for a while before finally settling in Agadir. Their house was modern, as was all Agadir, for the town had been completely destroyed by the disastrous earthquake of 1960 during which 12,000 people were killed in eight seconds.

"A man was killed in the very spot you sit," mentioned Jacquie nonchalantly, as I sat in a comfortable armchair sipping a red aperitif. A black-and-white photograph showed the spot all too clearly.

There was no warning shock, just a slip in the earth below the city, which drew a line across the city and jogged up and down once. Every building without steel supports for two miles on either side of the line collapsed like a pack of cards. No attempt was made to repair the city. The city was sealed away from the outside world by the military, while a rapid salvage operation was conducted. Survivors were few, and the only interment possible for the persons buried in the rubble was by bulldozer.

The old city can now be traced by the various hues of green that differentiate the buried streets from the buried buildings. The new city is built on virgin ground, and all buildings are of steel and concrete.

The Cadarses had been living on the third floor of one of the few substantial buildings in the old city when the quake occurred. The stairwell collapsed, and they had to scramble down rickety ladders to safety. They left their furniture where it was for six months, until their new house was built, and when they collected it, it was as intact as the day it had been left behind.

I later visited the Casbah with Joe Manivet. Originally,

Casbahs were castle fortifications, refuges that date back to ancient times when a Moor's castle was his only safe home. Nowadays, however, the Casbahs are the poorest parts of Moroccan cities.

At the time of the disaster, the authorities had not thought to look in the Casbah for a week. By then the place was unapproachable and rescue impossible. The quake had taken place just before midnight, when everyone was in bed, and even derelicts had taken shelter from the night's cold under the eaves of buildings.

Casbahs are built of clay and brick, which makes them too heavy should they fall in and too weak to withstand the shock. We went through the Casbah's gate, and all there was to see was a six-foot layer of rubble, spread evenly inside the Casbah's walls. A broken pot or two, a few ragged shreds of cloth, two or three memorial graves erected by relatives over the approximate site of the ruined homes and ragged white flags marking the spot where the family usually sat— that was all that remained of Agadir's Casbah.

My next day was spent removing everything dryable from the *Sierra Sagrada*. Clothes, books, bedding, life jacket, sails, ropes and papers—all were lined along the jetty. I dried the inside of my craft thoroughly with a piece of sponge rubber and sprayed it against the possible entry of the ever-present Sahara fly.

With everything running smoothly once more, I could attend to shopping and business in town. Among other things, I wanted to reprovision my now nonexistent food stock and to buy new parts to repair my still-broken mast.

I was returning from one of these shopping trips when Captain Skriver of the *Birthe Scan* came across to view the strange craft that had arrived. I put down my paper parcels, and we introduced ourselves: Captain Skriver was running his 1,500-ton ship along the African coast in my direction. He had just brought a cargo of poplar logs from Ghent, and after unloading at Agadir he would run in ballast to Dakar. His ship would be completely empty, and his decks completely bare.

"You are welcome to come along as a guest passenger," he offered, "and we have lots of room for the *Sierra Sagrada.*"

I jumped at his offer. Dakar was fully 1,000 miles away, and his lift would save me six weeks of motoring or sailing. Maybe I could even regain the time lost during my unexpectedly long ocean-crossing.

"When do you leave?" I asked.

"That depends on whether the moon is visible tonight," he told me.

It was the Arabic New Year of the year 1387. The Arabic calendar is regulated by the moon, and if the moon was not sighted tonight, then the New Year would be postponed for 24 hours. It made no difference if the moon was sighted someplace in Morocco. I assumed that holidays were also tied in with this, and if New Year was to be tomorrow, then the men would work overtime tonight.

It is most confusing. Sometimes the New Year starts in one country, and it is still the old year in all the neighboring countries. Some small communities even have two celebrations, if opinions are divided. Astronomy and science are ignored in this centuries-old rite.

It happened that the moon was sighted, and the *Birthe Scan* was unloaded. In haste to make the necessary arrangements before the holidays set in, I made the tour of the authorities for the second time in two days. This time it was for passport checks and export clearance to leave Morocco.

Once again the authorities gave me unimpeded cooperation.

My motor had not been overhauled as yet, nor had it been thoroughly drained of the water that had leaked into the pistons during the hoisting to the deck of the *Kostroma*. Rather than risk any further corrosion damage, therefore, I poured a cup of oil into each cylinder, resolving to attend to its repair upon reaching Dakar.

Before leaving Agadir I received a congratulatory telegram from Lois, of the Field Museum, plus a cable from the *Chicago Tribune* asking me to phone as soon as possible. Joe Manivet drove me to the post and telephone offices, and within minutes I was speaking to Bill Granger, the reporter who had been assigned to the story. We spoke for 35 minutes, and I just hoped it was understood the call was *collect* to Chicago. Otherwise, I would be in debtor's prison for a year or two as a penalty for not paying an enormous intercontinental phone bill.

Bill Granger told me that the *Tribune* wished to buy exclusive syndication rights of the journey. This suited me perfectly; I could not wish to work in cooperation with a finer newspaper. I filled in most of the details of the journey up to the time of my arrival at Agadir, and Bill said he would call back at four o'clock that afternoon to make final commitments and to fill in the details of what the conditions and rights would be.

With 15 minutes to spare I was waiting impatiently at the Somatime office, but my anxiety was needless. At 4:00 P.M. sharp Clayton Kirkpatrick, the managing director of the *Tribune*, assured me that I would receive more than sufficient cash to recoup my costs and still leave a healthy amount over to give Operation LAFF more than a smiling chance of success.

It was therefore with a light heart that I said good-bye

to my friends at Agadir and made myself comfortable aboard the *Birthe Scan*. My own typewriter was wet and partly rusted and was only the lightest of portables at best. The journey to Dakar was expected to take five days, which would be more than enough time to sort my notes and type them in tidy order. I borrowed a typewriter from Steffan Poulsen, the chief officer, and buckled down to work.

Captain Skriver, Steffan Poulsen, Engineer Paul Arne Bendsten and I all ate at the same saloon, and I must say I was fattening nicely after my long fast at sea.

Once more my cabin was in the ship's hospital. This was also my typing room, out of everyone's way. A notice on the wall intrigued me. *"Rum for 1 person"* the notice read, and I had visions of a habitual drinker having a standing order with the steward. However, it really was a government regulation to prevent overcrowding, and it meant, "Room for one person"—the sign was in Danish.

Before starting typing, I made an inventory of everything I had on the *Sierra Sagrada* and came to the conclusion that it had been a very successful craft. The sails for the Atlantic crossing were the original ones I had made in Cartagena some 18 months before. They had cost $11, the price of the canvas alone. They had been patched a lot, and the jibs were just about completely ruined, one of them having been blown into two separate parts and restored to half its size, but the mainsail and mizzen were in fair condition and in much the same shape as when I had started.

The mast and spars had been saplings of palo amarillo, a wood of excellent quality, and what it lacked in flawless beauty it more than made up in strength. An oddity of palo amarillo is that it seems constantly to be growing new bark. It was always a lot of fun when showing my craft to strangers to peel off a piece of bark, as if it were the most natural thing in the world, and soon to see another bark-scar take its place.

Termites had been in the saplings when I bought them, and these had reached their glory when the craft was on exhibit at the Field Museum. Powdered wood-dust droppings over the exhibit floor had exposed the fact that the termites had awakened from the dormant rest to which they had withdrawn on the salt-spray-exposed crossing of the Caribbean.

The museum authorities tried to reach their lair with chemical insecticides, but the wily termites refused to eat anything but the wood of the masts. A result of this was that the foremast had a pronounced "S" shape when I reassembled the rigging, and the mizzenmast had bent to such an extent it would have done justice to an Australian boomerang.

The *Kostroma* completed the job on the foremast when she tied that two-inch rope around the lower part, breaking the "S"-shaped mast in two. The mizzenmast suffered an equally unnecessary accident when I returned across the Atlantic the following year. *Careful—12 ft. 6 in. Clearance* said the bridge notice in the New Jersey Intra-coastal Canal. Then it was I learned that I had a height of 12 ft., 8 in.: a lightened *Sierra Sagrada* had three inches less clearance than the overburdened Atlantic-crossing *Sierra Sagrada*.

The rigging was the same baling wire I had previously used and only the ropes and the halyards needed to be replaced.

The canoes, sails, masts, wood and paint, anchor and chain, canvas, tar, compasses and tools used to make the boat from start to finish—which had been only a hammer, a saw, a wrench, a brace and a bit—all combined, including the purchase of the materials for the new pontoon to cross the Atlantic, had cost less than $450. Added to this was the cost of the motors and gasoline plus various truck transportation costs. These additional costs had run well over $2,000. But these later items were luxuries as far as I am concerned, for I still look upon the *Sierra Sagrada* as a sailing craft.

Bringing my notes up to date kept me busy. I had promised to get a newsletter to my friends in Chicago, and I hate to do things by halves. When I had finished, I had a fat 24,047-word newsletter for my friends and the *Tribune*, along with six carbon copies.

It took me 28 sleepless hours, from eleven in the morning to three the following afternoon, to finish the typing, and by the time I finished I was just about bushed.

By this time also we had reached Dakar harbor, and a reporter of the *Tribune* was there to meet me. He had flown out the day before, expecting to meet a bushwhacked mariner.

He was not mistaken. I was lying on the bed, fingers still sore after pounding the typewriter, thinking that two hours of sleep were nowhere near enough for someone who thinks himself cheated if he only manages to steal eight hours. My feet were high on a pile of pillows, for my feet and ankles had swollen as I sat all night on the hard hospital-cabin chair. Drinking half a case of beer and eating a two-pound box of chocolates may have helped also.

"Everything I ate must have gone straight to the bottom," I said, but the reporter did not think it funny. The weather was sweltering hot in Dakar, and he was pretty far gone himself.

We stayed at the N'Gor Hotel, a plush difference that

was pleasant for a couple of days, but I came to miss the compact straightforwardness of the *Sierra Sagrada.*

We went over the story's finer points and saw the town. The swelling in my ankles proved to be a minor vitamin-deficiency edema, soon cured by multi-vitamin tablets and healthy protein-rich foods. I even found the $280 in traveler's checks I had mislaid; they had been in the pocket of one of my jackets all along.

Finally the reporter returned to Chicago with the story. I stayed at the Pension Mon Loge for another week and then turned my attention to the next problem: preparation for my balloon attempt, Operation LAFF.

# Chapter XIII

FOR YEARS I had maintained that a balloon could cross the Atlantic by way of the trade winds with as much safety as any other craft. The winds are so reliable south of the Canary Islands that with a little steerage it should be possible to choose with fair precision the area in which one chooses to land. There are a number of stipulations, however. For example, I was not referring to complete free-flight, although I would like to experiment with this later: I was referring to a tethered balloon.

A trailing float would act as an anchoring device, preventing the balloon from becoming completely airborne. This float would also act as a pivot around which the balloon could be steered. Only the upper half of the balloon would be inflated, and the lower half would be pleated so that it would form an automatic sail. The resistance of the trailing rope would be just sufficient to slow the balloon enough to enable it to be steered. Such a craft had not been attempted before, to my knowledge. The more I thought of this idea, the more practical it seemed. Slowly, better and more fool-proof ideas evolved, but they always followed the same pattern.

The balloon would act as a kite or a giant sail. A round balloon may look more picturesque, but a flat side broaches better. A square balloon also would be cheaper to build and would have the advantage of *dog ears* that would be useful for tethering the steering ropes. Finally, a bridle could be placed around the balloon and attached to the trail-rope, and this could be manipulated for steering from the basket. I would be in this basket, sitting under the balloon, and at first I even considered using the kayak that I had carried on deck as a substitute in case a sufficiently large basket could not be procured.

The major obstacle to this plan was coordination. Logistical problems looked appalling. Ropes and basket and balloon and hydrogen somehow had to be assembled at one spot. This was the reason behind the *Sierra Sagrada*'s journey. Only by having all my equipment with me could I be assured that it would all arrive safe and sound, and this also had to fit into my budget.

Shipping costs by conventional means would have cost a fortune. I omitted mentioning the fact that calcium hydride is considered so dangerous when in moist surroundings that ships are reluctant to carry it without heavy insurance. "Just a little water and it goes *poof!*" said an insurance-shipping clerk. Maybe he was right. But at least I had my calcium hydride in Africa.

I had chemicals to make approximately 10,000 cubic feet of hydrogen, which in turn would lift in excess of 600 pounds in weight. And I had it figured out to the pound.

| | |
|---|---|
| 1 Balloon | 180 pounds |
| 1 Balloonist | 150 pounds |
| Basket & Rigging | 80 pounds |
| Food & Misc. Gear | 190 pounds |
| Total | 600 pounds |

The theory was beautiful. However, the more I experimented with chemical hydrogen, the less I liked it. I had been unable to obtain any accurate figures or even any opinions from chemists, physicists and other qualified people, and I was reluctant to approach the firm at which I had bought the supply, since this easily might have led to difficulties over complex import-export licenses. But my own primary experiments suggested that the temperatures would be well in excess of 500 degrees.

I took it for granted that my amateur knowledge had made me exaggerate the heat, for a well-known expedition had carried calcium hydride on a balloon journey, although the calcium hydride eventually was used as ballast only.

"If they can do it, then I can do it," was my reasoning. The other expedition had experts by the dozen. Surely they would not have carried calcium hydride if it was such a hazard.

I was wrong. The other balloonists were just damn lucky they did not blow their balloons sky-high. Calcium hydride is explosive; I'll explain more about that later.

No one crosses the Atlantic with a cargo like mine without a certain amount of apprehension. My most conclusive experiments were carried out at sea, using sealed test-jars that I had prepared in order to view deterioration similar to what probably would happen in the deck-cargo of sealed drums. When I poured a little chemical from one of the jars onto an industrial thermometer, the dial went up to its maximum reading of 380 degrees with a force that almost bent the needle.

However, with cash to spare from the *Tribune*, I now hoped to discard the chemicals and to purchase hydrogen cylinders instead, thereby cutting the inflation risks to zero. But I had much to learn. In particular, I was to find out, with increasing surprise, that money is a most useless thing when trying to buy such nonmercenary things as common sense, good judgment, reliability to get things done even when the highest prices are paid and down-to-earth and honest opinions.

At Dakar I made inquiries of a junior executive in an industrial gas company regarding the possibilities of shipping hydrogen cylinders direct from France. "It will take two months," he informed me, and later he would not even write a guarantee that two months would be sufficient time.

Other factors also looked unpromising. Although Dakar is the nearest African land to America, the wind consistently came too much from the north; this time both my pilot-chart and I agreed. Day after day the winds blew from the north, and the direction I required to set off was due northeast. If I had taken off into that north wind, the chances are that I would have been blown toward the Antarctic. In fact, the westerly winds of the southern *Roaring Forties* might even have taken me to Australia—a fascinating thought.

Now that I knew my position was too far south, I made plans anew to start up the coast once more toward the Canary Islands, reconnoitering for the most favorable take-off site. First, however, I had to have my Johnson outboard in proper running condition, and I made arrangements with a local repair firm to collect the motor for a professional overhaul. At the same time I had the *Sierra Sa-grada* ferried out of Dakar's main harbor to Henri Bassinet's marina, where I could bring my craft to seaworthy shape in sheltered comfort.

It was great to be on shore again, for I had no intention of putting out to sea at once. This was the first time I had been in this section of Africa, and my wandering instincts took hold. I prepared for a series of short loops: three-day journeys of 100 to 200 miles, with Dakar as my base.

Leon Siroto, of the Field Museum, had asked me to be on the lookout for artifacts of the Wolof or Mendingo peoples, and Gambia, an independent country, some 100 miles south of Dakar, seemed to be an excellent place to start. Gambia had once been a British possession, and many of the residents spoke English. Mendingos were the warrior-race of Africa, from the time of the old Ghana and Mali empires to more recent days.

Travel is comfortable along the West African coast, for the French-built asphalt roads were kept in good repair. Further inland the roads deteriorate to laterite, with a choice of either red dust or mud, depending on whether it is the wet or dry season.

Nowadays most Mendingos are agricultural, and they use the same tools and methods they have used for centuries. Soon mass production will take over, and the craftsmen will lose their skills, so I had hopes of buying a cross-selection of their tools before these skills were lost. I already had a fair knowledge of slash-and-burn agricultural techniques from previous travels in both South American and Asian countries, and I was keen to extend my knowledge.

My first stop was Brikama, a small groundnut-growing town that was divided into two principal family groups by the main street. The groundnuts had been harvested in late November and early December, and they were now being threshed for home consumption and market.

This was an excellent time to collect their hand-plows, hoes and other tools, for the equipment now would be put aside for six months until a new crop was sown, and the owners would have plenty of time to make replacements.

"Why do you want it?" the farmers asked, for even white men had to use a *dabadingo* for something.

If I had told them that I wanted them for a museum, the price would have skyrocketed.

"I am going to start a groundnut farm in Chicago," I jested. Before I knew it, they came to sign up as fellow workers on the project. Shamefacedly, I admitted why I was collecting them, but they did not believe me now, and soon I had a hundred people wanting to return with me.

The town chief got me out of the mess and also told the newcomers of the tools and implements I wanted. Soon a regular path was being beaten to my door by enterprising farmers who were only too pleased to trade in their wives' worn *dabadingo* plow for a brand-new, stronger one.

I collected a large sackful of these small but well-balanced hand implements before continuing past Brikama into Gambia's higher valleys. Local transportation took me along circuitous routes, until I arrived back in Senegal and Dakar.

It had been a fleeting journey, but an interesting one. Later, when I had more time and knowledge, I could journey further and gain a better overall picture of the countryside and of the farmers' economics. Just now my mind was still preoccupied with my sea journey.

On reaching Dakar, I placed the plows and hoes into

separate plastic bags and stored them between-decks. When I had time, I planned to catalogue them in more detail, but first I needed to bring back the *Sierra Sagrada* to sea-going order again.

Inquiries at the repair shop told me the motor was ready and repaired. We tested it out in the workshop's test-tank, and I was delighted to see how easily it started and how smoothly it ran.

"How much?" I asked, thinking that possibly the pistons, the bearings and all the gears had been replaced.

"You will have to ask the office," the mechanic said. "But these are the parts we replaced."

They were mostly ignition parts: a couple of coils, both sets of breakers and condensers and gaskets to replace the old ones after the motor had been stripped down and re-assembled. Labor costs are low in Dakar.

"Surely this will be only about $10," I thought, as I made my way to the office to pay the bill.

"$105 or the equivalent in West African francs," the cashier said, as he presented me with the bill.

It was all in code numbers and French, neither of which meant much to me. "There must be a mistake," I suggested. "Ignition equipment does not cost that much cash."

"We will have to keep the motor if you cannot pay the account," the clerk admonished.

I had no alternative except to pay this outrageous figure, but I did go to the manager's office and explain my position. He looked over the price list on the invoice and said that everything looked in order to him. "Prices of parts are high in Senegal," he said. "Taxes alone are often 200 percent of normal American costs."

I could appreciate this. Dakar is looked upon as one of the most expensive towns in the world. Income tax is almost zero, and the cost to run the many phases of government is borne almost solely by import duties. Gasoline costs four times the U.S. price, and the price of the cheapest shirt is between $8 and $10. Food is cheap, if grown locally, but everything else costs a fortune.

"If Johnson Motors will send replacement parts, we will refund the items penny for penny from the current price lists," the manager offered.

This was generous by any standards. I was later to learn that a simple error had more than doubled the cost, but at the time I was still baffled as to why the costs were so high. I sent a letter to John Tuzee in Waukegan, explaining the position and enclosing the list of code numbers and French names from my receipt.

I would have liked to have stayed around and waited for a reply, but with a running motor I could now make my way northward against the winds and continue my search for a balloon take-off site.

Now that the *Sierra Sagrada* was cleaned of barnacles and repainted, she looked as trim as ever. The broken mast-ends I joined together with a reinforcing section of three-inch diameter pipe, and I welded fittings to hold the gaff.

Henri Bassinet threw the mooring lines clear, and for the first time in a month I was once more on my own in the open sea. Unlike the grim North Atlantic, the sun was bright and shining, and I settled in comfort against the snug tiller.

# Chapter XIV

AROUND the old seaplane base I motored, past the imposing fortress of Goree and the main channel entrance to Dakar's modern harbor. I ran parallel with the coastal *corniche*, beyond Cape Verde and N'Gor village. Dakar is almost an oasis in Senegal's heat-seared savannah; once I had passed the airfield's open grounds, there was virtually nothing in front of me until I reached St. Louis, a few days' hard-driving time away.

A few isolated Wolof fishing communities lay cradled by sand dunes every fifteen or twenty miles. But these were virtually unapproachable by motored craft, owing to the scouring surf that persists regardless of the calmness of the day or of the otherwise apparent protection of offshore breezes.

White beaches stretched for mile after mile. Occasionally, fishing pirogues paddled in my path to gaze in awe at the twin canoes so similar, yet different. Wolof pirogues have special bows and sterns that give them the impression of medieval battering rams—an apt description, for the long-pointed false bow has been evolved to launch the canoes with a minimum of resistance through the violent surf conditions that prevail along West Africa's port-starved coast.

Some of the pirogue canoes were made of fibrous coconut palm, heavy and waterlogged when they had been at sea barely half a day. Others were made of ceiba: *fromage*, the Wolofs called it—a play on words, for in French *fromage* means *cheese*. *Fromage* wood is easy to carve—as easy as cheese, in fact. And, later, I was to buy one of these Wolof pirogues to replace my homemade pontoon.

"Fromage," they told me my new pontoon was.

"I hope you have no mice aboard," I told them.

Wolof fishermen kept me informed of what I could expect to encounter for the next few miles. "Keep close to shore," I was told near Cayor. "Rip-waves surge from a bottomless cut, which is less than a mile from the coast."

In this natural canyon, the underwater currents frequently ride straight up and down, as though on an elevator. And, incidentally, the currents mix plankton and weed to feed the fishes, thus making the ex-Queendom of Cayor a rich fishing community.

Once past this spot, I kept further out to sea. The Wolofs are not seafarers. They prefer to stay close to their own chosen villages, fishing for a few hours in the day or night and seldom venturing out when the sea is rough.

For millenniums fishermen have been on this coast. From one end of the Sahara to the other, from Mauretania to Egypt, scientists have found stone tools and bone harpoons and fishing hooks. The Sahara was once covered with tall trees and green pastures, and along this now barren coast unrecorded fishermen must have lived and loved and died.

Around 2000 B.C. there began a great natural change.

The climate gradually became drier; the Sahara received less and less rain; its rivers began to fail. Some fishermen must have remained, but others moved north and south. During these unrecorded times, many fishermen also must have been lost at sea, and the only place to which they could have drifted would be the Americas of today.

It is not known who these people were. The area I was passing is now the general southern limit of blue-eyed Berbers and the northern limit of African Negroes. What it was in 2000 B.C. is anybody's guess. But it was pleasant to think that the Santa Marta dugout canoe may have bridged a 4,000-year gap, for it was made by *zambos*, sons of slaves and descendants of people from these African shores.

I had at least expected an occasional protected beach or a natural island or two as I motored northward, maybe even a wharf in the towns the names of which I saw on my chart. But all I saw was endless sand and rolling seas. Even St. Louis, which looked so large on the map, possessed no harbor on the oceanic side.

Sometimes I passed commercial fishermen—Japanese, Spanish and Portuguese—who laid out endless miles of nets for shrimp or sardines. Since I was so close to shore, I had no problems of running into their nets, for they stayed well outside the three-mile limit.

At night I dropped an extra-long anchor and line, and I could hear the current swirling past the *Sierra Sagrada* as I was held in place. I had started with 84 gallons of gasoline on deck, and nearly half of this already was used. It seemed as though my attempt to motor to Port Etienne and the Canary Islands would be in vain unless I could buy plentiful supplies at such early ports as St. Louis and Nouakshott.

St. Louis gave me the answer. The town lay sprawled

along the oceanfront, but there was no sign of any safe place
to land. Even the local fishermen seemed to distrust it, for
there were few fishing pirogues to be seen.

I could have backtracked 12 miles and then have gone
up the St. Louis River to the shelter of the waterfront, but
it was clear that on the Atlantic seaboard it would take a
virtual ferry service to refill my diminishing gasoline supply.
I was further assured, by the solitary Wolof who was in my
area, that gasoline was even more difficult to obtain in
Mauretanian ports than it was on the Senegal coast.

It had taken me three days to cover the 100 miles to St.
Louis, and the thought of battling any further did not ap-
peal to me. Dismally I turned back, and in 36 hours I was
back at Henri Bassinet's marina. Henri welcomed me again,
and I made other arrangements to get to the Canary Islands.
It was still too early to expect many details from Johnson
Motors, but a telegram from John Tuzee indicated that the
parts would soon be on their way.

Motoring had not proved practical, but the *Alconville*
would be sailing to the Canary Islands in three days. The
great advantage of having portable craft is that they can be
frequently portaged, and I had no intention of making the
*Sierra Sagrada* an exception. I booked a passage on the
*Alconville* for myself, taking along the *Sierra Sagrada* as
deck cargo.

In Dakar I had made friends; 30,000 energetic French
people makes for a large society. An idiosyncrasy of tropical
colonial towns is that so many people invariably have
idiosyncrasies—indeed, this is one of the many fascinations
of the tropics.

I had met Erick Baumann before at a beach club. He
was in his late twenties, although how he had survived so

long is beyond me. An extrovert by nature, he combined the owning of a work-shocked jeep and trailer with a side occupation that took him frequently to France as an excellent steeplechase jockey. His family owned a large horse training and racing stable, which kept him in good practice. His girl friend at the time was Jocelyne, a mild-mannered secretary in the work week and a racer of souped-up Mercedes sports cars on the annual thousand-mile-around-Senegal *grand prix*.

Along with a friend I was invited to join them on a weekend pig hunt in the swamp northland adjacent to the Mauretania-Senegal frontier. "It sounds like a pleasant rest after that miserable journey along the coast," I thought.

Jocelyne drove the hundred-mile-plus trip along the inland asphalt highway to St. Louis, and apart from a few badly worn shocks and a steaming radiator, the jeep came through unscathed. Then Erick took over, and we left the asphalt behind and steeplechased across red earth and wide-open scrubland until we reached the meandering swampland of the St. Louis River, the home of the savagely tusked wild boar. However, after the ride, I felt I could face any wild boar without the slightest trepidation. My pulse returned to normal, and I was soon in my own element again.

I had left my little .22 Savage behind. It would have had little more effect than a mosquito on the tough hides of these brutes, and if there is anything worse than an angry boar chasing you, it is having an angry boar chase you when there are no trees to climb within 15 miles.

Erick had hired a Peul guide to help us through the lowland region, which accounts for thousands of square miles of this river-saturated scrub, and we tramped and splashed through sharp-pointed brush and grass after the elusive game.

In true French style, we came fully prepared, with

cheese and bread and bottles of red wine, so it was hardly an epic feat. In fact, it had more the air of a picnic than a chase. But it made us mad to see pigs by the dozen, erect, bristling tails waving high, as they kept clear of our noisy path and headed for more distant and quieter regions.

Weaverbirds and fishing fowl make the swampland a veritable garden. I had seen hippopotamus, elephant and gazelle by the dozen on my previous journey past Niokolo-koba, and I was more interested in photographing than in shooting, but we finally shot a few ducks for the evening dinner and called it a day. Our camp was near a Peul settlement, and I went there in search of artifacts.

The Peul (or Pullo, Fulani or Falah) are nomadic cattle herders who move around West Africa with a facile disregard of frontiers. Sometimes they settle in towns, where they have a reputation for being astute businessmen. But the cattle herders never have, nor seem to want, anything more than plenty of cattle and an overcrowded tent.

They sow millet broadcast and protect it from their herd. Groundnuts and maize they cultivate between their travels, and their diet is supplemented by fishing, birds and such roasted delicacies as rabbits and hedgehogs. For essentials, such as clothes and aluminum cooking pots, they must trade, but preferably without bartering their cattle.

This is where modern finance in the guise of foreign pig hunters and artifact-collecting tourists is harnessed to the full; for when I visited their small encampment, I paid more for one primitive plow than one Pullo would have paid another Pullo in years. An aluminum cooking pot, all our empty cans and bottles, a handful of West African francs, and a dollar or two in cash also changed hands. Our two-day stay at this remote thorn-bush camp made a desert millionaire of a usually destitute family.

Peul are Moslem; therefore they do not eat pig. Ahmed,

our guide, was only too delighted to lead us around to kill off this otherwise useless animal.

Walking had brought no positive results, and Erick decided to use his jeep as a horse. Early next morning, after uncoupling the trailer and leaving it at our old campsite, we went bounding over the plains in hot pursuit of any game we saw. The idea was to spot the pig, then go charging at full throttle alongside. My shotgun waved like a surrendering flag, but Erick could drive parallel with a pig and shoot it point-blank from a three- to four-foot distance.

Erick shot two pigs, but I do not think that I even scared any. My previous shooting had always been on terra firma, and most of the time in that jeep ride I was definitely airborne. From other points of view the journey was a great success, for although I had no pigs, I had used a full 20-exposure roll of 35 mm. Kodachrome.

We returned to camp, both satisfied. Jocelyne, who had a cheese and wine dinner in readiness at the campsite, was awaiting our return. Ahmed sat on the back seat, as enthusiastic as any of us and just as tired.

The weekend was over too soon. We rehitched the trailer, drove Ahmed back to his nomadic family and made our way along darkening tracks toward the main road. Hardly had we left the Peul village than we saw a sow and two plump porkers along her side. The temptation was too great to resist, and Erick threw off his lethargy and went bounding off the track after new game.

"Let them go!" yelled Jocelyne, with feminine anguish for the wild little family.

"Let them go!" I yelled, for I still had aches and pains from the previous chases.

I fired a couple of barrels at the porkers as they weaved their way around the bushes, but they were far too agile to give me time to aim. With a final "Yahoo" Erick put his foot on the accelerator, forgetting we had a trailer behind. Even when we were more than a foot off the ground, Erick was still gunning the motor.

We landed on all four wheels, but the trailer jackknifed and rolled over on its side. I managed to get a clip of .22's after the disappearing trio, but they were too far away for me to have much chance of success.

It took a couple of hours of hard work to unload the trailer, hammer the damaged bodywork back in shape and be on our way again. It had me worried, for early the next morning I was to catch the *Alconville* to Las Palmas. The *Sierra Sagrada* was already on deck, and I was ready to try the Canary Islands for my long-delayed balloon attempt.

# Chapter XV

ESTABLISHING myself in Las Palmas was a more difficult problem than I had anticipated. Finding a place to store the *Sierra Sagrada* occupied my first nine days, for marinas and other yacht facilities are unknown in the busy port.

At first I hoped to find a drydock berth in the Club Nautico, but it had recently moved to a new location, and although the new club site boasted an Olympic-size swimming pool, lounge, bar and spacious dining room, its boat-storage facilities were too small to allow the *Sierra Sagrada* to enter. It was not for want of trying, however, for the Club Nautico had 15 executives who tried their best to persuade each other to find room for my craft.

Finally, after a desperate week of returning *mañana* to see a different person, I was allowed a place on the flat parking lot outside the club's workshop. And it might all have ended had not the executive in charge of the parking lot belatedly realized that it was impossible to move in there, since a steep incline was in the way, and the *Sierra Sagrada* would surely slip and damage the craft below. Eventually, the best that could be done was to tie up the *Sierra Sagrada* in the oil-streaked bay at the opposite end of the harbor, under the care of a watchman's eye.

The nine days had not been completely wasted, however, for I had found a reasonable take-off site at Arguineguin, a small fishing village at the south end of the island. Once past the Canary Islands, I would have no obstructions or major shipping routes in my path for 2,700 miles. Normal trade winds should take me unimpeded across the Atlantic, leaving me with a whole, empty ocean in which to test the steering capabilities of my balloon.

This is the route that was taken by Christopher Columbus and by almost all the sailing vessels that followed him. Nowadays steamships and the convenience of the Panama Canal have made this route obsolete and abandoned, except by the dozens of small yachtsmen who yearly make the crossing.

Colonel Juan Carbo, second-in-charge of the Spanish Air Force contingent in the Canary Islands, was enthusiastic about my proposed balloon project. "Is there any way the Spanish Air Force can help?" he offered.

There definitely was. "Do you have a six-man tent I can use for a command post?" I asked.

"We will send you two," said Colonel Carbo, and, true enough, two tents arrived the next day at Arguineguin.

I made camp directly on the beach, under the shelter of a banana plantation's wall. One tent I kept as living accommodation, and the other I furnished as a workshop.

My only remaining concern was hydrogen, for I was still reluctant to use chemicals. With cash to spare I could afford to inflate 20 balloons, but cash was not of much use now, since I was close to a barrier of very nervous people who flinched at the thought of a balloon flight.

I made the rounds of importers and small industrial plants. "We have nitrogen, oxygen or acetylene," I was told. "But you will not be able to buy hydrogen on this island."

"Can I have it imported?" I asked.

"Impossible," they told me. "Hydrogen can only be carried from Spain in specially registered ships. Special licenses are also needed at the port of loading and the port of unloading."

"Maybe I can fly it out?" I asked in desperation.

"You can get no hydrogen on this island without the proper permits," I was told again, and rules and regulations were showed to me to prove that this was true.

A license for unloading would be a simple matter, but the formalities for loading the hydrogen in Spain were something I could not arrange. Transporting goods between the Spanish mainland and its far-flung island outposts needs a complex organization of agents and intermediaries.

Usually I get along very well with Latin government officials; they have a wonderful way of bypassing petty rules and regulations when they wish. But these selfsame officials have a unique knack for discovering new rules and regulations if they wish to be obstructive.

An officious attitude necessitates an official approach. Long ago I realized this truism. With apologies to the people who owned the letterhead, a completely fictitious *Eric L. Kelly* of the equally fictitious *National Exploration Soc.* and a nonexistent *Commodore Reimer*, I wrote myself a letter with my almost rusted typewriter.

April 6th, 1967

Dear Mr. Brenton:

Your balloon journey across Lake Michigan was perfect, and a remarkable achievement. The navigation surprised the committee, for you arrived exactly at Palo Alto pier as planned, and two minutes earlier than you had originally estimated.

Our club has offered $20,000 if you can cross the Atlantic using a similar method.

Our suggestion is that you fly at 80 to 100 feet across the Atlantic, instead of the 25 feet you used over Lake Michigan. You will agree that this will simplify navigation further, and you will only need 150 pounds of trail-weight, instead of the 600 pounds you used this last time.

One word of caution. The Federal authorities advised Air Commodore Reimer that an emergency radio transmitter must be carried while entering United States territorial waters.

As you are tethered to the sea, the Coast Guard regulations are the same as for normal craft. (Even though your craft is technically a balloon, this makes no difference.) Red light and green light must be carried for port and starboard and white light for aft. These can be carried on your gondola, and I suggest that an emergency light be trailed at the end of your trail rope.

As you will never reach a height of more than 1,000 feet (you will never reach a height of more than 200 feet), air regulations do not apply.

I am sorry we cannot forward the license. As you know, balloon licenses were discontinued in 1965. However, if any difficulties arise, please let us know. Commodore Reimer or I will be only too pleased to help.

> Good luck on your tremendous venture,
> Eric L. Kelly
> President, National Exploration Soc.

If no one else would give me official encouragement, then it seemed right and proper that I should give myself that encouraging letter that was meant to seduce the hardened hearts of rockbottomed officialdom.

However, when I showed this letter to newspapermen and officials to "prove" that this was an honorable and profitable enterprise, results were not exactly what I hoped. The feasibility of this journey was now "authenticated," but word swiftly spread among otherwise helpful people that this single project would make me a fortune.

"Rich men have many followers, but few friends," the Chinese tersely say, and the local people thought I was a millionaire. Most of my modest successes in travel are because I work on the same level as the people with whom I deal. Now I had to branch out on my own as I tried to push the balloon project through.

A month had passed since I had landed as Las Palmas. During this time I had assembled the basket-gondola, trail-line, food, emergency supplies and associated items such as a rubber life raft, camera equipment, walkie-talkies and similar accessories.

Inflating could not be delayed indefinitely. Last minute pleas to the authorities and to the local newspaper people for importing hydrogen had not brought any results. The last big obstacle I had not been able to overcome, and apprehensively I turned my attention to the calcium hydride.

Even my most cursory experiments had shown that rapid generation of hydrogen from calcium hydride was too hazardous to attempt. But to generate hydrogen slowly I would need to anchor my balloon securely, for winds can blow strongly and steadily in the Canary Islands, and a half-filled balloon could easily burst apart or be blown adrift.

An old idea, frequently used in Europe, was to inflate in the shelter of a large building. This method was used for inflating transportation and passenger balloons during the famous Paris Siege of 1871 during the Franco–German War, and the same method was used for many of the smaller airships that predated regular airplane flights.

However, there was no building in Arguineguin capable of holding a balloon with a bulk of 50 feet square and 20 feet high. So I built one.

It was definitely not a solid building. This was a scaffold type of structure, 50 feet long and 30 feet wide, which would wedge the balloon tightly when inflated until I could release it into the wind. Four of us erected the building in one strenuous day, while the people of Arguineguin gasped at their newly acquired suburb.

Cars and trucks came and went as new equipment was bought and transported. Having to generate my own hydrogen was something I had anticipated, but I had hoped that it would never happen. It was to be my final effort, and soon I was to find it was indeed a most conclusive final effort.

Juan Carlos Lascaray organized most of the purchases. Besides being a private in the Spanish Air Force, he was also a successful businessman. Military service is compulsory in Spain, and at the time when Colonel Carbo assigned him to me, Juan had only eight more days of service before again being a civilian.

The eight days ran out as preparations were nearing the initial inflating attempt, and Juan was back in civilian clothes once more. But Juan still remained on the project. "Ask Juan" was always the answer when purchases were needed. Plastic, basket, camping equipment, transport, scaffolding and many other items: Juan knew where to buy them. He also bought them cheaper, thereby saving the project a great deal of expense. Black plastic, 200 feet long and 20 feet wide, was attached to the scaffold walls, and other lengths were stretched on the ground in the form of a groundsheet. All were held in place with ten-foot lengths of wild bamboo, cut from a nearby swampy grove. We rehearsed a take-off plan and made arrangements for an emergency stand-by crew of fishermen plus a local fishing boat.

If only I could have bought proper hydrogen cylinders, inflation of the balloon would have been no problem at all. My first attempt to use the chemicals fizzled prematurely. I half-filled a thick plastic bowl with 15 pounds of calcium hydride, and attached a two-foot-diameter plastic sleeve to the balloon neck. Through a flexible hose I poured a quart of water into the bowl, to begin the process. Hydrogen gushed almost instantly into the balloon at first, then the heat mounted and the plastic bowl melted into a sticky mess.

The heat reaction had been so intense that the bamboo poles showed signs of smoldering. I had used plastic to reduce the risk of accidental sparking, but obviously the heat was too intense for plastic to be efficient, and I postponed any further attempt until I could build sturdier equipment.

Next I tried an iron pail set below the surface level of the ground. The water tube was led high into the scaffold for greater pressure—and also to give a generous measure of safety in case of backfire. Once more 15 pounds of calcium hydride was used, and this time I managed to pour more than a gallon of water into the still before a deep-throated roar and an explosion whistled through the air like a shotgun blast. A second and larger explosion rocked the balloon, and then it went up in flames.

Jim Holmes, my assistant at Arguineguin, wielded the fire extinguisher while I kicked the burning plastic to one side. We were both more shaken mentally than physically, for we knew, of course, that there was potential danger involved in the attempt to inflate the balloon and had prepared ourselves to meet it.

Spectators gawked over the dividing barrier as we fought the flames under control. Too dangerous an explosion could not have occurred, for I intended to manufacture no more than 500 cubic feet of hydrogen in the balloon and then to use secondary bags to transfer the remaining gas to the balloon. But even a few hundred cubic feet of hydrogen can cause a most uncomfortable boom. It is a shame I did not practice on my secondary bags first, for the balloon was badly charred.

The thing that I feared might happen had happened. Later I realized in more detail the pattern of chemical sequences that had occurred.

As the oxygen in the water and air was absorbed by the calcium hydride, the free hydrogen became instantly hot and absolutely bone-dry. Just two crystals fracturing or rubbing against each other would act like a tiny spark plug; a pailful of tiny crystals acted like a pailful of tiny spark plugs. Months of planning had come to naught. Possibly I could repair the balloon, but I still had not solved my inflating problem.

One watchman proudly walked around Arguineguin saying he had been blown off his bicycle by the force of the explosion. Before he had gone past the first tavern both he and his bicycle had been blown in the air. And within an hour he was explaining to friends how he had been blown over the 15-foot-high plantation wall adjacent to the balloon.

"He'll be an astronaut in a few weeks," said Jim sourly.

Sadly I made preparations to break camp. Then, just when the project was at the lowest ebb, a couple of reporters came to my tent and said, "Frank, we've found hydrogen for you."

"It's a little late," I said negatively.

It seems that CINSA, a local chemical factory, was releasing 96 percent pure hydrogen into the atmosphere as a waste gas. This is the very thing I had been asking for during my stay in the Canary Islands. Charitably, I assumed that I had not been told about it simply because everyone thought that I already knew of the source.

The CINSA factory was near the sea, and a pipeline could easily be run to the beach. It certainly seemed practical. The beach was presently being used only as a sand and gravel pit. One-ton boulders and water-filled holes gave it a raw moon-cratered appearance, but doubtless a 60-foot-square area could be cordoned off and leveled.

In its favor as a take-off site, moreover, were the 100-foot cliffs behind the beach, which would act as a perfect wind-break, and suitable water less than 30 yards from shore, which would anchor an auxiliary launch adequately. The beach's small size was a hazard, but it was certainly the most encouraging place within practical reach of the factory.

First, however, before the attempt was made, two novel ideas had to be worked out. A hydrogen pipeline would need to be run 1,000 feet from the factory to the beach. And since I was at the northern end of the island instead of the southern, I would need to be towed into the favorable trade winds by an auxiliary launch.

Once more a succession of trucks and cars wound its way to my campsite, taking the equipment from Arguineguin to the CINSA site. Everything except the scaffold building was moved.

Winds are so strong and frequent in the Canary Islands

that most banana plantations are surrounded by high walls. Beneath another of these high walls, therefore, I pitched the tents for the new campsite, overlooking the part of the beach quarry that looked most favorable.

A thorough inspection of my balloon suggested that I ought to have a new one made. The ocean waves and salt water of the *Sierra Sagrada* crossing had done no harm, but the few seconds of fire in the explosion had charred more than 100 square feet of plastic. It would be faster and cheaper to build a new sac than to try to repair the old one, so I phoned Houston explaining my position.

Time was now the all-important element. Already it was nearly three months since my *Sierra Sagrada* crossing was completed, and the Caribbean hurricane season would soon be starting. I would have to move fast. This time I told Griffolyn Plastics the reason for my balloon. Within ten days they had fabricated a new bag for me and sent it on its way. By the time it reached the CINSA beach, the site was leveled and prepared.

Jim Holmes had continued on his travels after the first balloon failure at Arguineguin. He was now on his way by ship to South Africa. I missed him, but before leaving he had introduced me to Pete Weiland, and Pete became my new offsider. What Pete did not know about balloons he was willing to learn, and we got along splendidly. We certainly needed to, for the second attempt suffered from more problems than the first.

All my life I have traveled alone. In this way I can keep projects strictly controlled yet sufficiently flexible to drive whatever way events may lead. The more people involved in a project, the more chances things will go wrong, or so it seems to me. Thus, the balloon launch was a new and, because of its complexity, potentially very difficult experience.

Simplicity is the main ingredient in all my journeys. But in this case, it was not to be simple. In fact, there was a definite case of too many cooks spoiling the broth on the CINSA beach.

To start, however, all went well, as the inflation and launch procedures were carried out.

### INFLATION

1. Before inflation is started, secure the balloon with a plastic protection cover, which will also act as a housing.
2. Ensure that the balloon does not inflate to a height of more than 20 feet while under canvas.
3. Check to see that all balloon and ground attachments are in their expected final positions—including gondola/basket, bridle and controls, trail-rope, and takeoff ballast.

### EXPECTED TAKE-OFF PROCEDURE

4. Trail-rope to be led toward shore and laid in snag-free position.
5. Towrope to be anchored on deck of waiting launch.
6. Make last-minute check of all equipment and attachments before take-off. Check to see that the offshore launch's engine are operating and idling smoothly.
7. Release balloon with tethering ropes cut along plastic protection cover, allowing the balloon to raise directly into the wind.
8. Launch will proceed at cautious speed to vicinity of take-off winds.
9. Release towrope.

After all these things were checked, I would be on my way. I had walkie-talkie communication sets to work between the crew on the ground and myself in the balloon-basket, but communications were poor in other directions.

Pete Weiland had been to the *Oficina Meteorologia* at

the Gando Airport, and he had received the bulletins of
expected surface winds covering a seven-day period:

| | | |
|---|---|---|
| Mar. 30 | NNW | 15 knots |
| Mar. 31 | N | 20 knots |
| Apr. 1 | NNE | 15–20 knots |
| Apr. 2 | NE | 15–20 knots |
| Apr. 3 | ENE | 20–25 knots |

April 3rd was today's date, and the following two days'
forecast was:

| | | |
|---|---|---|
| Apr. 4 | ENE | 20–25 knots |
| Apr. 5 | ENE | 20–25 knots |

The forecast was excellent. Since we were on such a large
island, we had no way to check our own weather, since
mountains protected us from the winds from the shore.
But these winds also affected the winds from the sea, and
our weather knowledge depended on accurate and favorable
information.

We started inflating at one o'clock on April 3rd, and I
expected to be on my way within eight hours, thus making
the most of the cool night breezes to help carry me away
from the shore. My balloon was half-inflated before the bad
news reached me that my offshore launch had been canceled
and had been replaced by a large deep-sea tug.

"Surprise!" I was told. "We've got a bigger and better
take-off boat."

It was more than a surprise; it was a positive shock. The
deep-sea tug could not reach anywhere near the take-off
coast and had to stand by nearly a half-mile away.

Pete and I already had our hands full keeping our project under control. Tourists began swarming into the camp.

For days I had been trying to persuade some of them to stay at the camp with me for the take-off; now they came in hundreds—and I had made the inexcusable error of trying to expand my take-off team.

Instead of assisting, they made the whole project twice as complicated. One tourist proceeded to unwind a 250-yard coil of heavy nylon safety line from the wrong end and tangled it in such a knot that it took three fishermen two hours to untangle it. Another tourist turned my hydrogen valve higher, "So you can get away faster." Fortunately, I caught him in time and shooed him away, closing the valve to normal again.

Two girls served coffee and snacks from the camp store as the evening turned to night. They were the only tourists who seemed to know what they were doing.

A stage of the journey that seemed to be taking an inordinate length of time was that of transferring a rope to the deck of the deep-water tug. The Spanish government's ships are not always well supplied, and I finally learned that they did not have sufficient line aboard, so they decided my safety line would make an excellent substitute.

Besides not having a safety line to leave my basket in a hurry or to pick up ballast from the sea, I also had to wait a couple of hours for the new line to be looked at and stretched and for a conference to be formed regarding the best way of taking the line from the shore to the tugboat.

About midnight everything seemed under control. "How are things, Pete?" I asked. He gave the O.K. sign. We had done everything we could.

Finally, I checked all the parts, and everything seemed to be perfect. There was one section of plastic that would need to be cut away to allow the bridle of the balloon to rise clear, and Pete would take care of that. Side ropes would have to be cut by tourist helpers.

I clambered aboard the basket and yelled, "Let her go!"

Pete cut his tethering plastic perfectly, but an assistant on another group of ropes hesitated too long, and the balloon ripped its way forward out of control.

What should have been a smooth upward flight was changed into a fabric-tearing drag as the balloon oozed to escape the encircling girdle rope. This dragging motion broke the hydrogen conduit, adding the deafening roar of high-pressure gas to the chaos of a fleeing take-off crew.

This hesitation in cutting one rope virtually spelled the end of the journey. I should have kept to the original idea of cutting the balloon free myself, hauling the balloon down and then clambering aboard the basket later.

"We can't let you go like this, Frank," someone had rushed over and said.

Now 80 pounds of cover sheet had torn apart and caught on the balloon's peak. Pete attempted vainly to drag the cover clear, but it was caught too securely. This plastic groundsheet and cover had been my old burned-out balloon, which I had cut lengthwise to protect the new one. Cutting the proper girdling rope would have allowed the cover to open wide, allowing the balloon to drift away free. The dragging motion had impaled the torn cover on the balloon's peak in the manner of one bag inside another bag.

Before I could go any further, this 80 pounds of excess plastic would have to be removed. Pete quickly saw this and organized a group of tourists, reporters and CINSA officials to haul the balloon down, while I stayed in the basket directing operations.

The offending plastic came off all too suddenly. The effect was to make the balloon bag swing wildly, recoiling in an arc in much the manner of a gigantic punchball. As it reached its furthest swing, the basket and I were jerked with a pendulum motion off the ground and out to sea.

It happened too fast to keep control. Colonel Carbo, who was standing behind my basket, was knocked into the water. The basket hurtled onward, smashing into a high outjutting rock and throwing me overboard. The lace of one of my shoes caught momentarily in a sliver of the balloon's basket, but I kicked myself clear and scrambled ashore.

The take-off crew ran forward, and helping hands rushed the colonel to the hospital. I limped behind, leaving the balloon forgotten in the speed of the tragedy. Or almost forgotten, for I looked back and saw that the balloon was perfect as it headed out to sea.

"Like a giant white genie," Pete called it.

The balloon design and the project were perfect; only logistics had beaten me.

# Chapter XVI

SLOWLY I returned to America. Certainly I should not complain, and yet the whole trip had not really been a success.

Colonel Carbo had been badly shaken by the accident, but doctors assured me that there was nothing more seriously wrong than extensive bruises. Normal care and a strong constitution would have the colonel on his feet again in a matter of weeks.

Pete remained with me until camp was broken. The camp equipment was returned to the Spanish Air Force, and the *Sierra Sagrada* was made seaworthy once more.

The abandoned balloon had proceeded out to sea under its own power, at the end of the towline. It seems as though the weather bureau had been in error with its forecast, and an offshore wind had blown northwest instead of northeast. The tug's captain, not realizing that there had been an accident, towed the balloon three miles out to sea before finding that there was no one aboard; he then brought the balloon back to the CINSA dockside.

At the dockside I inspected the balloon for damage and

checked the chances for a third attempt. The balloon itself was in fine condition, but the gondola/basket was so broken that I could walk into it sideways. Many of my emergency supplies also were ruined.

The chances of further cooperation by the authorities were now zero, but the hydrogen-filled balloon could not be left where it was. I would have to release it. As the tug churned at 15 knots on its return journey to the naval station at Las Palmas, Pete and I cut the straining balloon free. It soared high in the sky, leveling out at an altitude of about 10,000 feet, traveling Africa-bound.

However, the authorities decided that the liberated balloon represented a hazard to air traffic. Consequently, at about midday on Thursday, April 4th, over the sea and about 35 miles south of Jandia beach in Fuertoventura, jet fighter planes of the Spanish Air Force shot it down.

It was not the finish to the project as far as I was concerned, but it was certainly a dramatic postponement. A compact team would be necessary the next time, along with a little audacity plus a little drive: surely not an impossible combination.

I made a new set of sails for the *Sierra Sagrada* and headed south 900 miles to Dakar. Along the barren Sahara coast I checked new sites, but none seemed as encouraging as the northern islands.

At Dakar I was welcomed back by Henri and Arlette Bassinet, and I at last replaced my old plywood outrigger with a 22-foot Wolof fishing pirogue. With this new outrigger I would make faster time on my Atlantic trip to America. The old pontoon was still seaworthy, and I traded it in as part of the cost for the hospitality of Henri's marina.

My replacement parts had arrived in Dakar from John- son Motors. It was now that we accounted for the costly error for what proved to be a $12 repair job. Two tubes of *C* oil and one of *A* grease had been charged as two *cartons* of *C* oil and one *carton* of *A* grease—a total of 36 tubes instead of three. A couple of other bearings also had been added in error.

The repair agency magnanimously took these parts back. In fact, there had been a steady retail inflation over the past three months, and I received $125 instead of the $105 I had paid! By now my old spirits were more or less return- ing, and I saw nothing wrong in having an excellent repair job done and making a $20 profit.

May 31st, 1968, I headed back across the Atlantic on an uneventful return voyage. The journey took me 47 days, and my new, unloaded *Sierra Sagrada* was so light that she steered by herself, giving me less than six hours of watch on the tiller over the whole journey.

I stayed four days in St. Croix, revisiting friends made during a six-month stay some years before. It was a lazy trip, and I made my way from island to island. Someday, I vowed, I would make this journey with the square-balloon system, and the scudding clouds above seemed to agree.

Along the Bahama Islands, I touched at ports most nights. Sometimes I would run on a sandy beach and explore a cay or anchor in a coral-fringed cove and go snorkeling or browsing. The *Sierra Sagrada* was perfect for this type of activity, and I was loath to finish the voyage.

The miles and months went by, uneventful but pleas- ant. I passed the length of the sheltered Bahamas, running along the canal-lined Florida coast, past the eastern states' canals and oil-laden New York port, then up the Hudson River and Erie Canal to Lake Ontario and, finally, the Trent Canal to Lake Michigan and Chicago.

Dick Newick, a friend of mine in St. Croix, had asked: "Frank, what will happen to the *Sierra Sagrada* when you reach Chicago?"

I really did not know.

"Maybe I'll sell her, Dick," I'd answered.

"But you've already half-sold it twice," he'd pointed out logically.

Holy mackerel! It was true, even though they had been separate outriggers.

I had best watch my step; that was tricky territory. I had best stay on strong, safe ground for awhile.